Edward H. Bennett   Architect and City Planner, 1874-1954

Joan E. Draper

The Art Institute of Chicago 1982

Lenders to the Exhibition

Mr. and Mrs. Edward H. Bennett, Jr.

City of Cedar Rapids, Iowa

City of Chicago, Chicago Park District

City of Chicago, Department of Development and Planning

City of Chicago, Department of Public Works

City of Minneapolis, Records Management Division

City of Pasadena, California

Kelmscott Gallery, Chicago

Anonymous Lender

This catalogue is published in connection with the exhibition "Edward H. Bennett: Architect and City Planner, 1874-1954," organized by the Art Institute of Chicago and presented March 4 - July 4, 1982.

Both this catalogue and the exhibition it accompanies were supported by a grant from the National Endowment for the Humanities.

© 1982 by The Art Institute of Chicago. All rights reserved. Printed in the United States of America.

Library of Congress Catalog Card Number 82-71084

ISBN 0-86559-048-6

Designed by Michael Glass Design, Chicago, Illinois.
Typeset by Dumar Typesetting, Inc., Dayton, Ohio.
Printed by Rohner Printing Company, Chicago.

Cover: Edward H. Bennett, designer, Michigan Avenue Bridge, 1920.

Contents

Lenders to the Exhibition	2
Foreword James N. Wood	4
Acknowledgments John Zukowsky, Joan E. Draper	4
Edward H. Bennett: Architect and City Planner, 1874-1954 Joan E. Draper	7
Abbreviations	43
Notes	43
Catalogue	49
Appendix: List of Bennett's Work	58

Foreword

In September 1981 the Board of Trustees of the Art Institute of Chicago voted to establish the Department of Architecture, the museum's 11th curatorial department. Using as its base the enormous collection of architectural drawings in the Burnham Library of Architecture, this new department, under the direction of John Zukowsky, Associate Curator in Charge, will collect and exhibit artistic works—drawings, models, and fragments—as opposed to manuscript materials. As every scholar knows, however, manuscripts contain a wealth of historic data which are essential for the accurate interpretation of artworks. As in the past, the Burnham Library will continue to collect architects' manuscripts when they are relevant to existing collections at the Art Institute. Such was the case with Edward H. Bennett's papers, an outstanding collection of archival materials that complements the library's extensive holdings of diaries, letters, and memorabilia of and about his mentor, Daniel H. Burnham. This archival material has been especially useful in that it contains photographs of Bennett's drawings that, unfortunately, are no longer extant.

Burnham's reputation in city planning of the early 20th century is so widespread that it overshadows the achievements of others who were instrumental in disseminating the City Beautiful Movement throughout America. In this exhibition catalogue, *Edward H. Bennett: Architect and City Planner, 1874-1954*, guest curator Joan E. Draper, Assistant Professor, University of Illinois at Chicago Circle, surveys Bennett's career and discusses his impact on our cityscapes. She has created a welcome documentation of Bennett's work that is a fitting sequel to our exhibition catalogue *The Plan of Chicago: 1909-1979*. We hope that this catalogue and the exhibition it accompanies will make the urban observer aware of Bennett's contributions to our present environment.

James N. Wood
Director

Acknowledgments

In 1953 and 1973, Edward H. Bennett, Jr., donated a substantial collection of his father's papers to the Burnham Library of Architecture of the Art Institute of Chicago. We are indebted to him, since this collection and the important objects now on loan from Mr. and Mrs. Bennett form the basis of this exhibition and catalogue. A 1980 Faculty Summer Research Grant from the University of Illinois at Chicago Circle enabled Joan E. Draper to undertake a preliminary investigation and cataloguing of the Bennett papers. Continuation of research and the realization of this exhibition and catalogue were made possible through a grant from the National Endowment for the Humanities. We are grateful to the university and the NEH for their funding support. Likewise, we thank the following people for their assistance throughout the project.

At the Art Institute, a number of people helped us: Anne Stern, in the Development Office; John Mahtesian, in Museum Photography; Robert V. Sharp and Susan F. Rossen, the Assistant Editor and Editor, respectively, of Publications; Barbara Mengel, head of the Volunteer Office; Reynold Bailey, Coordinator of the Art Installation Department; Timothy Lennon, Conservator; and Wallace Bradway and Mary Solt of the Registrar's Office. All deserve special thanks. We also commend volunteers such as Sally Eastman, who assisted in cataloguing the collection, and Yuri Nakazawa, who assisted in research. Susan Deremo and Janet Rogatz were research assistants on the project, but it was Sura Levine who, as the primary research assistant, did a superb job in uncovering a wealth of data on Bennett and his works. Others were most generous with their time and information: Thomas Martinson of Minneapolis, George Gurney of the National Museum of American Art, and Chicago architects Paul McCurry and Vincent Viscariello.

Finally, we are grateful to the following people who helped expedite our work by promptly replying to our research questions and requests for loans and photographs (all are located in Illinois unless otherwise specified): E. C. Alft, Elgin Historical Society; Gary F. Baeten, Land Use Administrator, Fort Wayne, Ind.; Myron B. Barnes, Seneca County Museum, Tiffin, Oh.; Patience H. Brewster, Domestic Archivist, The Society of Merchant Venturers, Bristol, England; Joseph Butler, Department of Public Works and City Architect, Chicago; Robert Buechner, Village Manager, Winnetka; Lillian Casten, Joliet Public Library; the staff of the Chicago Historical Society; Louis P. Chrzasc, Bureau of Engineering, Department of Public Works, Chicago; William P. Coburn, Berkeley, Cal.; Phil Cole, Retired City Engineer, Evanston; Michael Corbett, San Francisco, Cal.; Cathy deLorge, formerly with the Oregon Historical Society, Portland; James Dillon, Cartographic Division, National Archives, Washington, D.C.; Lincoln Donaldson, Engineering Department, Gary, Ind.; David Gebhard, University of California, Santa Barbara; Eleanor M. Gehres, Denver (Col.) Public Library; Leslie Heumann, Pasadena, Cal.; Rebecca Hill, Tiffin-Seneca Public Library, Tiffin, Oh.; Robert H. Irrman, Archivist, Beloit College, Beloit, Wis.; David A. Johnson, University of Tennessee, Knoxville; Karen Kingsley, Tulane University, New Orleans, La.; Sue Kohler, Commission of Fine Arts, Washington, D.C.; Karol A. Koon, Bureau of Planning, Portland, Or.; Greg Koos, Archivist, McLean County Historical Society, Bloomington; Dick Kvach, Department of Planning and Redevelopment, Cedar Rapids, Io.; Joseph D. LaRue, University of Chicago; Dennis J. Latta, George Rogers Clark National Historical Park, Vincennes, Ind.; Gregory Lennes, Corporate Archivist, International Harvester, Chicago; Kevin Leonard, Northwestern University Archives; Cynthia McClelland, Princeton (N.J.) University Archives; William McClung, Chief Engineer, Chicago Park District; Pauline S. Miller, Official Historian of Orange Co., Toms River, N.J.; Austin Moller, Archives, City of Portland, Or.; the staff of the Municipal Reference Library, Chicago; Donald Nollar, Housing and Community Development, Pasadena, Cal.; Robert J. Piper, Directory of Community Development, Highland Park; Puerto Rican Tourist Office, Chicago; Mary Radmacher and Dorothy Rasmussen, Skokie Public Library; Mary Reecer, Planning Department, Elkhart, Ind.; Don Salyer, Department of Planning and Redevelopment, Cedar Rapids, Io.; Kevin L. Sarring, Harry Weese and Assoc., Chicago; Ann Scheid, Housing and Community Development, Pasadena, Cal.; Marlys Svendsen, Community Development Department, Davenport, Io.; Beverly Swanson, Municipal Information Library, Minneapolis, Minn.; Ed Uhler, Chicago Park District; Thelma Vanderberg, Librarian, Regional Plan Association, New York City; Walter Welsh, City Clerk, St. Joseph, Mo.; Elizabeth L. White, History Division, Brooklyn Public Library.

John Zukowsky	Joan E. Draper
Associate Curator in Charge	*Assistant Professor*
Department of Architecture	*University of Illinois at Chicago Circle*
The Art Institute of Chicago	

Edward H. Bennett: Architect and City Planner, 1874-1954

by Joan E. Draper

Edward Herbert Bennett (fig. 1) was born in 1874, the son of an English master mariner, who sailed out of Bristol. At the age of 12, Bennett began his training in Bristol at the Merchant Venturers' School, an early technical school founded out of concern for education in the applied arts and sciences that the Great Exhibition of 1851 had awakened in England. Bennett probably took drawing and modeling classes and may have studied geometry, building construction, and the other technical and scientific courses the Merchant Venturers' School offered.[1] Perhaps following the advice of cousins in Florida, his father decided that Bennett should become a rancher in California. But after his arrival in San Francisco in 1890, the young man followed his own inclinations, and by 1892, he was working for architect Robert White, a designer of residential and small commercial buildings.[2] More important for the young immigrant's future, however, was the influence of Ralph Bernard Maybeck, the brilliant, eccentric architect whose Berkeley home became the gathering place and informal school of the best aspiring talents in the days before any architectural school existed in California. In this circle Bennett met Willis Polk and Arthur Brown, Jr., who would later be his colleagues, and Mrs. Phoebe Apperson Hearst, the philanthropist. Her many contributions to architecture included the scholarships she gave to the students whom Maybeck had inspired to attend the Ecole des Beaux-Arts in Paris. Among the recipients were Bennett, Brown, and Julia Morgan, the first woman to enroll in this most prestigious architectural school.[3]

When Bennett began his studies at the Ecole des Beaux-Arts in 1895, the Paris school was a mecca for Americans seeking the disciplined and scholarly training it provided for anyone who could pass the stiff entrance exams. H. H. Richardson, Louis Sullivan, and Charles McKim had studied there, and so would scores of the leading American architects of Bennett's generation. Under the tutelage of architects Julien Guadet and E. J. B. Paulin and the older students in their Beaux-Arts atelier, Bennett learned the art of composition: that is, to design buildings by combining elements from various historical sources into unified and orderly wholes.[4] He entered the school a skilled watercolorist, although, by his own admission, one too preoccupied with the pictorial and decorative aspects of architecture.[5] Thinking broadly and working from the general to the specific, principles taught by the Ecole, would stand Bennett in good stead in his future career as a city planner.

Thanks to the preservation of Bennett's letters to a San Francisco friend, we know something of his life during these student years in Paris. Unfortunately, few original drawings survive; others are known through photographs (fig. 2). Bennett entered many of the competitions by which students advanced through the curriculum. In 1896, he submitted drawings of the Royal Portal and the north right portal at Chartres Cathedral for an archeological *concours* (cat. no. 3). Design projects that year included a savings bank and a royal bedchamber. But no student in Paris spent every day working in the studio. Bennett's letters report dinner parties and sketching trips with friends from San Francisco and with Peirce Anderson, who would leave Paris for Chicago in 1899. Other Paris friends included Georges Fernand Janin, who was later invited to Chicago to assist with the Plan of 1909, and Arthur Davis, the London architect and partner in the firm Mewès and Davis. Frequent visits to relatives in England, among them an architect cousin, also broke the routine. In fact, Bennett spent two years between 1897 and 1899 working for an architect in London.[6] After his return to Paris and while working toward his diploma,

Fig. 1
Edward H. Bennett, c. 1920. Photo: Matzene.

Bennett entered several competitions sponsored by the Royal Institute of British Architects. In 1901, his watercolors earned him an honorable mention in the Owen Jones Studentship competition—and the jury's comment that his work was merely clever. His deficiencies apparently having been rectified, he won the competition's 1902 prize of £100, which was to be used for "a tour of not less than six months duration [for] the improvement and cultivation of [the candidate's] knowledge of the application of color as a means of architectural expression."[7] In the company of two friends, Bennett visited Italy, Sicily, Athens, and Istanbul.[8] His small pencil sketches of buildings in Genoa, Siena, Bologna, and other cities (see cat. no. 5) are typical of the travel drawings of Beaux-Arts-trained architects. Accurately recording the characteristic details of historical structures, these facile sketches were generally more effective than a photograph for capturing an idea or element that could find its way into a future design.

An ambitious young man with a newly minted Beaux-Arts diploma could look forward to a bright future, especially if he chose to settle in New York in 1902. Certainly, Bennett must have known that the big architectural firms in the cultural capital of his adopted country were eager to hire skilled draftsmen expert in the academic classical style. He himself soon found work in the office of George B. Post. Post was a leader in his profession and head of one of the largest and most respected offices in the country, with such commissions to its credit as the Manufacturers and Liberal Arts Building of the 1893 World's Columbian Exposition in Chicago, and numerous hotels, houses, offices, and public buildings. During Bennett's year-and-a-half tenure with Post, the firm designed the New York Stock Exchange. Exactly which projects he worked on is unknown, but ledgers in Post's papers indicate that between September 22, 1902, and March 31, 1904, Bennett's monthly salary of $150.00 was among the highest paid to the 50 draftsmen in the office during those years.[9]

Early in 1903, Post agreed to "loan" Bennett to Chicago architect Daniel H. Burnham, who had been asked to enter the competition for new buildings at the United States Military Academy at West Point and needed someone to work out his ideas. Peirce Anderson, Bennett's friend in Paris and Burnham's chief designer, suggested the collaboration.[10] Thus began a nine-year, mentor-protégé relationship between the two men. Bennett was soon to be launched on his career as a city planner under the wing of the architect who gave the new profession much of its luster.

The West Point competition provided Bennett his first opportunity to plan a huge complex of monumental and utilitarian buildings in a real setting. He later described his initial visit to the site:

> I shall never forget meeting with Mr. Burnham in New York, our early breakfast, our visit to West Point . . . and the novel experience of outlining the problem first hand on the site. A natural axis existed. While waiting for the train, Mr. Burnham spoke in his eloquent and convincing way about the famous Piranesi print which he described to me and its meaning in terms of Gray's Elegy.[11]

For Burnham, who had only recently completed plans for the redesign of Washington, D.C., and was still refining the Cleveland Civic Center Plan, the West Point project was another demonstration of his conviction that the orderly development of such a significant institution could take place only according to an axial plan.[12] The Burnham-Bennett scheme (fig. 3), a Baroque fantasy culminating in a gigantic version of the Chapel at Anet (Philibert de l'Orme, 1549), was totally idealistic, ignoring existing structures and the picturesque landscape of the Hudson River valley. The architectural critic Montgomery Schuyler indirectly accused some of the competitors, including

Fig. 2
Edward H. Bennett, preliminary sketch (unlocated) for the Concours Godeboeuf, December 6-21, 1901, for *"Une Rampe en fer et bronze pour l'escalier d'un Palais"* (a banister of iron and bronze for a palace staircase).

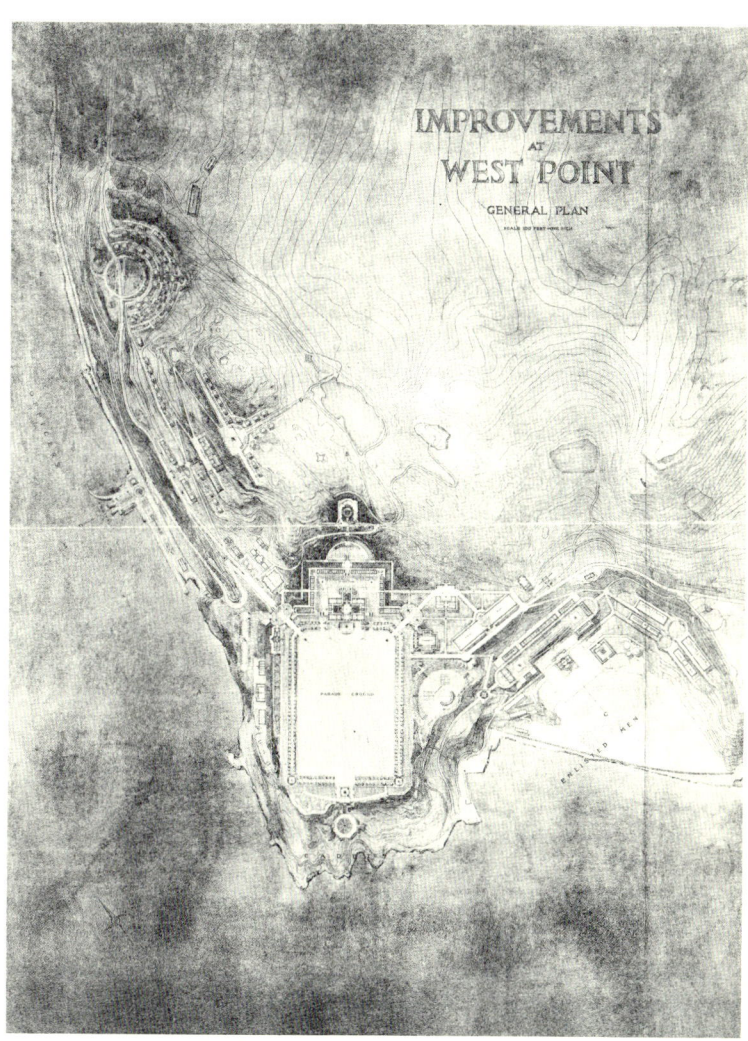

Fig. 3
D. H. Burnham and Co., Architects, *A Competitive Design for the Improvements at the U.S. Military Academy, West Point, N.Y.*, rendered by Edward H. Bennett, 1903. Published in *The American Architect* (September 19, 1903), pl. 1447.

Burnham, of taking the competition less than seriously and of treating it "as a kind of concours for a new and cisatlantic Prix de Rome."[13] His comments were altogether justified. In its grandiosity, formality, and reliance on French Baroque and other classical sources, the Burnham-Bennett plan resembles designs submitted to this ultimate Beaux-Arts competition. Although the jury consisted of George B. Post, Walter Cook, and Cass Gilbert—themselves practitioners of the prevailing classical modes—first prize went to Cram, Goodhue and Ferguson for their ruggedly picturesque, Gothic scheme. The outcome was almost a foregone conclusion, given the force of West Point's Gothic tradition. Burnham knew this and had entered the competition only as a favor to his friend Elihu Root, Secretary of War. It is possible that he used this rather futile exercise as a means both to perfect his own planning skills and to test the suitability of his temporary employee for an even larger planning scheme. The day after the West Point drawings were due (May 10, 1903), Burnham wired former San Francisco Mayor James D. Phelan: "[I] would consider making design of general improvement of your city if given single charge of it."[14]

But work on the San Francisco plan did not begin in earnest until September 1904. Bennett returned briefly to New York, only to be called to Chicago to join Burnham, who had taken immediately to this "poet with his feet on the earth."[15] The Chicago firm thereby gained a second Beaux-Arts graduate. Bennett was put to work designing new buildings for Chicago's South Park District. This commission, which came to Burnham and Co. in January 1904, was an important one for the city, the firm, and for Bennett. It came about as a result of agitation by settlement workers and reform-minded business and professional men concerned about the lack of parks and playgrounds in the city's poorest and most crowded tenement districts. Legislation was passed allowing the acquisition of new park land for the first time since the park districts were founded in 1869-70. The call for municipally supported playgrounds had been sounded throughout the country, beginning in the late 1880s. The South Park Commissioners may have responded somewhat late by national standards, but they acted more quickly and generously than their counterparts in the West and Lincoln Park Districts. Olmsted Brothers, the Boston landscape

Fig. 4
D. H. Burnham and Co., Architects, with Edward H. Bennett as designer, Fuller Park Fieldhouse, Chicago, 1904-11.

firm, laid out the 14 new small South Side parks, and Burnham's firm designed fieldhouses and other architectural features in 11 of them. Both offices were working simultaneously on improvements to Washington Park and the South Park District headquarters there. Both had long-standing connections to the South Side system. Just how many of the new park buildings, which were completed between 1905 and 1911, can be attributed to Bennett alone is impossible to determine, but he seems to have designed at least the facade of the Administration Building in Washington Park (now DuSable Museum of African-American History) and the fieldhouse at Fuller Park (45th and Princeton) (fig. 4). Obvious similarities of design and materials among all the structures suggest a single controlling hand. They are simple, classically composed and detailed structures, mostly of a rough-textured concrete. These buildings, among Bennett's few strictly architectural works, were praised in playground literature of the day. Several authors referred to Sherman Park, Davis Square, and the other new facilities as "country clubs" for the poor.[16]

Bennett's first real opportunity to learn about city planning came in September 1904, when he accompanied Daniel Burnham to San Francisco to begin work on that city's plan, one of the first comprehensive schemes for an American municipality. The experience was excellent training, and the responsibility delegated to Bennett indicates the trust his employer placed in him. After a few weeks of touring, surveying, photographing, sketching, thinking, and discussing, Burnham left for the Philippines to make plans for Manila and Baguio. Before departing, he had laid out the broad lines of the scheme. Although he returned to advise again before the plan was completed in September 1905, the detailed studies, presentation drawings, overall coordination, and report writing were left to his assistant. In November, when discussing the publication of the report with James Phelan, its chief sponsor, Burnham asked that Bennett be given complete control: "No one can take Bennett's place in this work, not even I."[17]

In San Francisco, Bennett encountered working conditions similar to those he would find later in his career. He and Burnham were responsible not to an official body, but to a private group, the Association for the Improvement and Adornment of San Francisco, founded in 1904 by reformer James Phelan and other public-spirited, wealthy civic leaders. The architects' task was to combine various individual public improvement proposals advocated by Phelan, such as an extension of Golden Gate Park, with their own ideas and those of other local men, into a comprehensive vision of a beautiful and commodious city (figs. 5, 6, cat. no. 12). The intended purpose of the resultant plan was manifold: to guide municipal investments in parks, streets, and public buildings, as well as private donations of monuments and buildings; to inspire public support for tasteful beautification; and to advertise San Francisco's virtues to the world.[18]

Responding to Phelan's vision of a socially, politically, and aesthetically reformed city, Bennett's imagination soared. With the draftsmen in his charge, he drew an ideal city, including such practical suggestions as the reservation of hilltops for parks, but unrealistically calling for a drastic reordering of street and land use patterns. A new civic center, over a mile from the retail center, was to be the focus of a network of new diagonal and ring streets. Despite his six-year residence in San Francisco and the assistance of Willis Polk and Association members, Bennett, like Burnham, remained an outsider. Both men were merely consultants, and Burnham an unpaid one at that. They were called to a city which had no planning commission, few resident architects interested in planning, and no planning constituency other than the Association. The fate of the Burnham plan was further compromised when Phelan engaged in a virulent

Fig. 5
Plan of the City of San Francisco..., from
Daniel H. Burnham and Edward H. Bennett, *The
Plan for San Francisco* (1905).

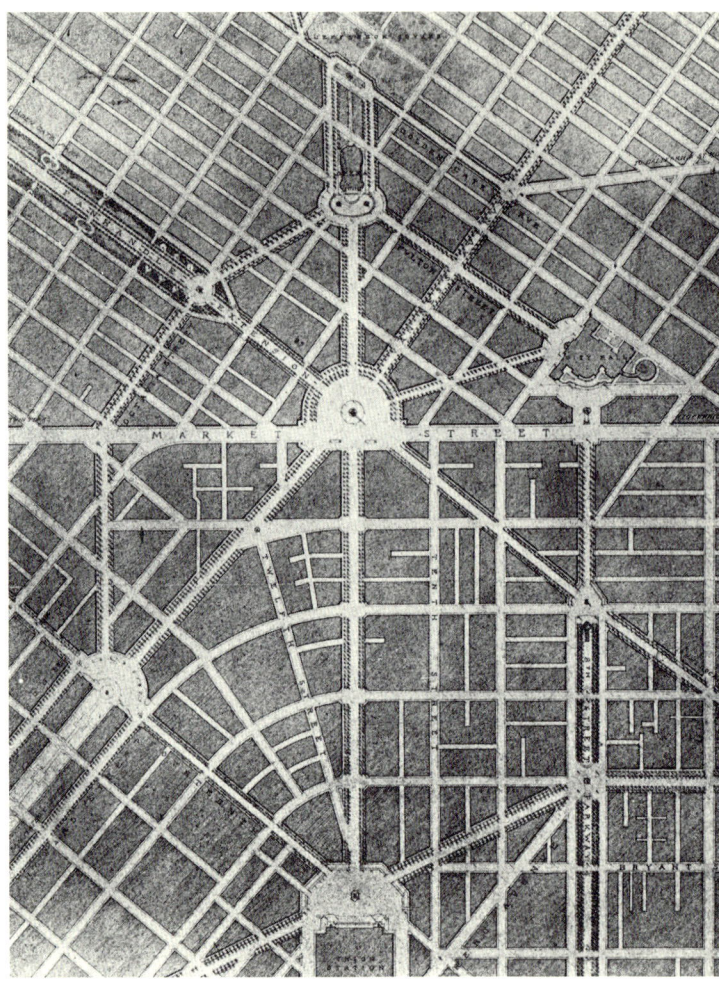

Fig. 6
Edward H. Bennett, renderer, *Plan of the Civic
Center,* from Daniel H. Burnham and Edward H.
Bennett, *The Plan for San Francisco* (1905).

war against corrupt municipal officials, which, unfortunately, discredited him and his civic improvement schemes along with those he attacked. Even the earthquake and fire of April 1906, which leveled 512 central city blocks, did not, in the end, create a golden opportunity to rebuild along new lines. That summer Burnham and Bennett returned to San Francisco to assist the Committee on Reconstruction in working out a street widening scheme based on their 1905 plan. Burnham gave advice and encouragement but soon returned to Chicago, leaving his assistant to work on drawings in the city engineer's office. Despite the more pragmatic character of the new scheme, it had no influence on the rebuilding of the city. Legal and financial powers were insufficient, and the tremendous distrust among political factions precluded its execution.[19] Nor did attempts by Bennett and Polk to revive their civic center scheme in 1909 and 1912 produce tangible results. When a center was constructed between 1912 and 1915, the design by other local architects kept more to the existing street grid, and its location had nothing to do with any comprehensive city plan.[20] This frustrating pattern of events was to be variously repeated throughout Bennett's career, albeit without earthquakes. The consulting planner had to entrust his scheme to his client and depart. When that client had no official status, the result was often merely a book of inspiring words and pictures.

Fortunately, Bennett's next big job with Burnham amounted to much more. In September 1906, the two men began studies for a plan which would set the standard for other cities to emulate. The Chicago Plan, a landmark document commissioned by the Commercial Club and published in July 1909, was a labor of love for Burnham, whose last major planning effort it would be. As for Bennett, who again took charge of the drafting room, it was to launch him on a long career as one of America's foremost planners of the second generation. After 1906, his employer declined numerous requests to repeat the efforts he had made for Washington, Cleveland, San Francisco, Manila, Baguio, and Chicago. Replying to the mayor of Holyoke, Massachusetts, Burnham wrote, "I do not care to be engaged any further in the planning of cities, except as to my own town, in which I have been engaged to help out."[21] In this instance, he recommended that the mayor of Holyoke seek out Boston's Frederick Law Olmsted, Jr. But after 1909, once the Chicago Plan was nearly complete, Burnham directed to Bennett all inquiries from the civic leaders of Portland, Detroit, Minneapolis, Cedar Rapids, and other American cities. From this time on, the young man's practice had less to do with buildings and became increasingly independent of D. H. Burnham and Co., although he continued to work part-time on the firm's jobs, such as the addition to Marshall Field's State Street store and the South Park fieldhouses.

Equally as important as these referrals were Bennett's involvement with the leader of the new profession and his introduction to the powerful men of the Commercial Club with whom he would later make the plan a reality. Unlike the majority of schemes produced in the first decades of the century, the Chicago Plan was in large part executed through the continued efforts of its creators, Bennett among them. From January 1913 through August 1930, he served as Consulting Architect to the Chicago Plan Commission. This position and the friendships he developed with important Chicagoans would lead to equally important commissions in New York and Washington. Whether large or small, every Bennett project displayed the influence of the Chicago Plan.

The elements of the Chicago Plan and the story of its making are well known and need only be summarized here. Essentially, the text and drawings describe a coordinated set of public works designed to modernize and beautify a city which had grown from village to metropolis so fast and with such a lack of foresight that congested streets, tangled and redundant rail lines, foul housing, and lack of open space threatened to strangle continued progress. In a collec-

Fig. 7
Chicago. Railway Station Scheme West of the River Between Canal and Clinton Streets, Showing the Relation with the Civic Center, rendered by Jules Guérin, 1908. Pencil and watercolor on paper. Published as plate 122 in *The Plan of Chicago* (1909). The Art Institute of Chicago.

tion of clear and splendidly rendered maps and drawings, the artists under Bennett's direction illustrated the ideal Chicago of the future (fig. 7). The main features of the plan were a metropolitan park system, a reordering of railroad tracks and terminals, a scheme for reorganizing lakefront and river facilities, a coordinated street and highway system, and the siting of new public buildings in relation to other improvements. These recommendations were not only backed up by careful study of existing conditions, but also made in reference to the entire region within a 60-mile radius of the city's center. The legal means for their implementation were considered as well.

The first step toward a comprehensive plan for Chicago had been taken by Daniel Burnham when he studied ways the city could preserve the grounds of the World's Fair of 1893, for which he served as Director of Works. Gradually, he interested Chicago's wealthiest, most powerful, and public-spirited men, members of the Merchants and Commercial Clubs. Fired by his vision and their own desire to improve the city's economic, civic, and cultural life, the two groups merged in late 1906 to sponsor the plan. For two years, led by Charles D. Norton, Charles H. Wacker, Frederic A. Delano, and Walter Wilson, Chicago's most prominent merchants, bankers, and capitalists headed the various committees that helped Burnham and Bennett gather data and deliberate alternatives. Not content to let the product of their hard work go unrealized, the planners cultivated politicians throughout the process and had the final illustrated report sumptuously printed and sent to everyone who mattered. In July 1909, shortly after the document had been published under Bennett's painstaking supervision, Mayor Fred A. Busse appointed the Chicago Plan Commission. This 328-member group included many of the most active members of the recently enlarged Commercial Club, as well as Chicago aldermen and others representing a broad range of civic interests. Charles Wacker, Vice-Chairman of the Commercial Club's Chicago Plan Committee, became Chairman of the 28-member Executive Committee.[22]

During the years he served the Chicago Plan Commission, Bennett also developed a substantial private practice and a national reputation as a city planner. By 1912, he had executed or begun planning projects in seven other cities:

Brooklyn, Cedar Rapids, Detroit, Minneapolis, Ottawa, Portland, and San Francisco. That year he employed about a dozen draftsmen, including—as Burnham had done for the Chicago Plan—a Frenchman "imported" to make renderings. Until Burnham's death, these men often helped with the older firm's work; in return, Bennett's office got help when needed.[23] After 1912, the operations appear to have become entirely separate. Nevertheless, old connections persisted. William E. Parsons, a former Ecole des Beaux-Arts student during Bennett's years there, joined the Bennett office in 1914 and in 1919 became a partner. Between 1905 and 1914, he had worked as Consulting Architect for the Philippine government, where he designed a number of buildings and implemented the plans of Daniel Burnham, who had recommended him for the job.[24] Parsons undertook many of the firm's design projects, while Harry T. Frost, an employee since 1912 and partner after 1922, assisted primarily with technical matters, especially zoning.[25]

The Bennett firm was engaged primarily as architectural and city planning consultants and did very little design work like that of architects in ordinary practice. When involved with architectural projects, its members often served in an advisory capacity or worked with sculptors or engineers, as in the case of the Pasteur Memorial (fig. 8). Thus, its members were professionally something of an anomaly. Although Bennett and Parsons, later Bennett, Parsons and Frost, was recognized as an established and prominent firm, the partners did not participate in many Chicago architectural activities. Before devoting himself entirely to planning, Bennett had run an atelier, whose student members included some of his own draftsmen, and in the 1920s Parsons headed one for the Chicago Architectural Club. Both belonged to the American Institute of Architects, but were only moderately active in the local chapter.[26] Compared to the architectural profession, firmly established with its own schools, licenses, associations, and code of ethics, the city planning profession was still in a formative state. The term "city planning" was hardly known before 1900, and the first association of practicing professionals was not founded until 1917. Bennett was one of 52 charter members of the American City Planning Insti-

Fig. 8
Edward H. Bennett in his office with the members of the Pasteur Memorial Committee, c. 1925. The memorial was sculpted by Leon Hermant in 1928. Originally sited west of the Field Museum, it was moved in 1946 to a park adjacent to the Cook County Hospital, 1835 West Harrison Street.

tute, the ancestor of today's American Planning Association. But the Planning Institute had a very shaky first few years. Only a dozen of its original members were engaged in actual plan making, and none except Bennett was from Chicago. Even by 1935, when he had almost retired, the national organization had only 120 members.[27]

Burnham and Bennett were pioneers when they made plans for San Francisco and Chicago. But after 1909, neither Bennett nor executives of the Chicago Plan Commission advanced much beyond the highly effective formula they created for carrying out the recommendations of the plan. The Chicago Plan became a sort of civic bible—a fixed record to be completed over the years. In contrast, as city planning historian Mel Scott has written, "the leaders of the emerging city planning profession . . . took the long view of urban problems and understood that there was more to planning than carrying out a specific scheme, no matter how grand."[28] Planning had to be flexible and to encompass more than public works. Bennett did not have the vision of Frederick Law Olmsted, Jr., who as early as 1911 warned that a city plan was not a set of architectural drawings but rather a piece of administrative machinery to be modified continuously.[29] Bennett's view remained very much that of the architect-planner. In certain respects, he continued to uphold the principles of the City Beautiful Movement, that first phase of American city planning between about 1900 and 1910, when new parks, diagonal boulevards, and symmetrical civic centers modeled after those of the great cities of Europe, especially Paris, seemed the answer to every city's problems. Unlike Olmsted and other pioneers of the teens and '20s, Bennett did not enlarge the scope of the profession beyond the Chicago Plan model by writing treatises and teaching in the new university programs. He was, however, a thoroughly competent professional who kept up with changes wrought by other men. He never became involved in housing reform, but he was an early advocate of zoning, transportation planning, and regional planning, three new activities that preoccupied planners between 1910 and 1930.[30] Although he continued to design civic centers and to be concerned with the aesthetic aspects of public buildings and landscape, much of his later work involved preparing zoning plans and sorting out street and rail systems within and between cities. Bennett's theory of city planning, if it can be called that, is embodied in several general articles and in addresses he gave to various associations. They reveal that he saw the city as a continuously expanding organism which could be given a perfect and essentially static order by the city planner. The purpose of a well-conceived street system and a properly framed zoning ordinance was to guide every urban function into its correct place. Although he repeatedly stressed maintenance of property values, Bennett's viewpoint was not that of a pragmatic technical assistant to his businessmen clients. His approach to planning remained in essence aesthetic, as a 1923 article reveals:

> The finest purpose of city planning is to create a beautiful setting for human life and activities, to plan the setting of everyday life as well as those suited to great public events. . . . In planning our cities it is well always to have in mind the truth of the Greek saying: "To make our city loved we must make our city lovely."[31]

Bennett attempted to put these convictions into practice during the 20 years he worked for the Chicago Plan Commission. Although he saw more of his recommendations executed in Chicago than in any other city, his influence was limited by the circumstances under which he and the Plan Commission executives worked. His associates on the Commission constituted a semi-official, quasi-public organization, created not by ordinance, but only by councilmanic resolution. Not until 1939 did the Commission have official standing in the city bureaucracy. Its powers were only advisory. Through 1920, the Commercial Club contributed more money to its operation than did the public purse.[32] According to Walter D. Moody, appointed Managing Director of the Commission in 1911, the arrangement stemmed not merely from the city's parsimony, but from the conviction that "city planning [is] a thing apart, to be kept distinctive from city government."[33] Accordingly, the Commercial Club provided Bennett's salary, at least until the 1920s. On January 28 and 29, 1913, eight months after Burnham's death, he met with Walter Wilson, Charles Wacker, and Joy Morton, "regarding the future operation of Plan work." They regularized what had been since 1909 an informal arrangement. Bennett was to be paid a salary of $7,500 a year for his Chicago work, which seems to have occupied at least half his time. He would continue to occupy the penthouse office atop the Railway Exchange Building where the plan drawings had been made. The Commission would pay the rent and the draftsmen's wages for Chicago Plan work. Bennett was also given permission to place "Consulting Architect to the Chicago Plan Commission" on his letterhead.[34] Although his salary fluctuated and Bennett later moved his office to Jackson Street, the arrangement remained relatively constant until 1930, when his position was abolished and replaced by an advisory committee.

The staff of the Chicago Plan Commission worked under the assiduous direction of chairman Charles Wacker in two mutually dependent operations: publicity and technical matters. While Bennett oversaw the drafting room on Michigan Avenue, Walter Moody ran the educational and promotional division out of the Commission's headquarters in the Hotel LaSalle. The success of Burnham's plan was in large part due to the efforts of this super-salesman Since the Commission had solely advisory powers, it could effect its projects only by persuading both the City Council to pass ordinances and the voters to approve bond issues. Shortly before his untimely death in 1920, Moody wrote *What of the City? America's Greatest Issue—City Planning. What It Is and How to Go About It to Achieve Success*, in which he explained his purpose and methods:

> It is hoped that [this book] may help establish a national conception of city planning and to firmly fix in it the factors of education and promotion. These must go forward, hand in hand, and first, before city planning results can be had. In America, the ballot box must go before the city planner.[35]

Moody's and Wacker's publicity efforts ran the gamut from the serious to the gimmicky. They included a popular version of the plan, distributed free to property owners; a textbook for Chicago's school children; scores of illustrated pamphlets on individual projects and issues, sent throughout the city and the world; hundreds of professionally prepared slide lectures; countless conferences with city, state, and federal officials; press releases to periodicals; the film "A Tale of One City"; and the proclamation of Plan of Chicago Day during which pastors preached its virtues.[36]

The consulting architect had less of a public role than did Moody and Wacker, although the drawings produced in Bennett's office illustrating such projects as Michigan Avenue (figs. 9, 10) and Wacker Drive (figs. 11, 12) helped officials and voters visualize the proposals. But attractive renderings were only a fraction of Bennett's output. Much of his and his staff's time was spent working out detailed designs for the Plan Commission projects, which were then executed by various other agencies, including the Board of Local Improvements, the Bridges and Harbor Division of the Department of Public Works, the Sanitary District, and the South Park District. All technical and design work was done by Bennett's staff until 1920, when Hugh E. Young was appointed to set up a separate engineering office. Charles Wacker, in a speech

Fig. 9
Drawing (unlocated) of the proposed Michigan Avenue Bridge, Chicago, from the southwest, c. 1912, by Bennett's office for the Chicago Plan Commission.

Fig. 10
The Michigan Avenue Bridge, soon after it was completed in May 1920.

made to the Commission upon his retirement on November 4, 1926, succinctly described the complicated design process that began with a motion by the Commission to undertake a particular improvement project:

> From its inception until the present, the Plan Commission has followed this invariable rule of procedure. First we make a thorough study of a contemplated improvement. We have always sought constructive criticism of our plans, and whenever suggestions have been made that other studies have shown to be better than our own ideas, we have cheerfully adopted those suggestions in substitutions for our own original ideas. Next the technical staff submits to me a joint report signed by all the associated technicians. . . . This report is then submitted to the executive committee, where it receives painstaking, able and thorough consideration. If the improvement is favorably passed upon by that body, it is then presented to the entire Plan Commission for official approval. When this has been given, our recommendation is submitted to the mayor and the city council for action by whatsoever municipal agency may have jurisdiction. After all this has been done, the Plan Commission stands firm upon its recommendation and places upon those in authority the responsibility for making changes, if any are made.

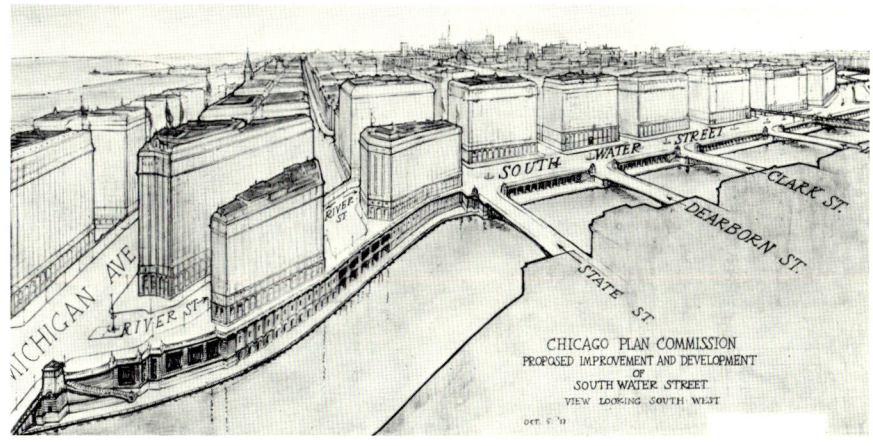

Fig. 11
Edward H. Bennett, the Chicago Plan Commission's South Water Street (Wacker Drive) design (unlocated), dated October 5, 1917, though not completed until 1926.

Fig. 12
Bennett, Parsons and Frost, a drawing (unlocated) of Wacker Drive as completed 1924-26 showing proposals for the eventual bridges over the Chicago River at Wabash Avenue (1930), State Street (1949), Dearborn Street (1963), Clark Street (1929), and LaSalle Street (1928). The Dearborn and Clark Street bridges replaced structures that already existed when the drawing was made.

In the same speech, Wacker praised the technical staff for its thoroughness and skill: "Our people have accumulated vast knowledge of the city. We are often called upon for information not exactly in our area because city officials know it is accurate and unbiased."[37]

The Monroe Street Bridge (fig. 13), completed on February 22, 1919, provides an example of the complicated negotiations Bennett undertook on behalf of the Chicago Plan Commission in order to assure that the aims of the plan were upheld. Unlike most of the other bridges the city built across the Chicago River during his term of office, this one was partially paid for by the Union Station Company, which agreed to fund a number of public works projects, including straightening the river, in return for the Council's approval of the Union Terminal Ordinance in March 1914. Monroe Street had had no bridges; now it could become a major east-west artery and another link in the Plan Commission's scheme to relieve traffic congestion in the central business district. Furthermore, the bridges constructed across the south and main branches during the teens and '20s were part of a massive riverfront improvement scheme outlined in the Burnham Plan. Although Bennett and his staff had prepared a number of earlier bridge designs, including the first version of the Michigan Avenue Bridge in 1910, the Monroe Street Bridge design, begun in 1914, was made by the Bridges and Harbor Division of the Department of Public Works. But Bennett had approval rights, as did the City Council's Committee on Rivers and Harbors, the Sanitary District, and the federal government. The bridge engineers proposed a single leaf bascule bridge 200 feet long. Bennett protested, calling for a double leaf trunnion bascule bridge of a shorter length more in harmony with the design for the Jackson Street and Madison Street Bridges, which he and the engineers had already completed. The architect was particularly aggrieved, since in 1910 he had held a series of conferences with bridge

Fig. 13
The Monroe Street Bridge (1919) from the southwest in late 1981. Photo: Bob Thall.

engineers and others concerning the width of the river channel and the aesthetic quality of new improvements. Bennett and his staff had developed a standard design and by 1912 had secured the promise of the Commissioner of Public Works that his department would follow the architects' suggestions regarding both the treatment of bridge houses and the location of trusses as far below bridge decks as possible (see cat. no. 14). The two groups had collaborated willingly and with good results. Now it appeared that the Association of Commerce and the Sanitary District had persuaded the engineers to deviate from the established scheme. The design was ultimately revised to conform with Bennett's model with the aid of the American Institute's Municipal Art Society, although its members claimed all the credit.[38]

After drawings for bridges, streets, or buildings left the Plan Commission's jurisdiction and made their way to the executing agency, the process was far from complete. As Wacker had indicated, changes could still be made before the final ordinance was passed by the City Council. Then, in the case of street widenings when property was taken, there began the lengthy legal proceedings for condemnation and determination of assessments, as required by Illinois law. These took years and cost millions. Michael Faherty, Mayor William H. Thompson's President of the Board of Local Improvements, which oversaw all projects involving the assessment of property owners, reported to the Commission on March 16, 1916. He told them that progress was slow on the 12th Street (Roosevelt Road) widening, one of the first Chicago Plan improvements approved by the Commission in January 1910. The bond issue had passed on November 15, 1912, but construction had not yet started. Faherty complained that red tape imposed by reformers made the legal proceedings "very cumbersome":

> It costs more to conduct . . . business now than it would if the business could be conducted on strictly business principles, even if occasionally someone did graft a little. . . . I am convinced that if I was permitted to run the Department I am the head of and did not have to consult lawyers I could save the taxpayers of Chicago a million dollars a year.[39]

Faherty was new at the job; by 1928 he would be convicted along with Mayor Thompson and the comptroller of illegal payments of $1,232,279.23 to real estate appraisers in return for political contributions. The Commission winked at this corruption of the system in order to push the work along.[40]

At the same Commission meetings to which Faherty had reported, the assistant corporation counsel told of the many challenges by property owners to the condemnation and assessments for the widening of Michigan Avenue from Randolph Street north to the river (see cat. no. 15). This improvement, along with the bridge, had been approved in 1911, but was not completed until 1920. Roosevelt Road was widened as far east as Michigan Avenue only by 1930. Restricted to an advisory role, the Chicago Plan Commission members, officers, and staff could do little but wait. Thus, although it is possible to say that Edward Bennett designed the architectural features of Chicago's most beautiful public works, he always collaborated with others and rarely supervised construction of his Chicago Plan work. As consulting architect, he played a role necessarily different from that of an architect in private practice.

If Bennett had to sacrifice control, he gained in terms of the scale of his work. Between 1912 and 1931, the City of Chicago raised $233,985,000 through bond issues and $381,446,834 through special assessments for public improvements.[41] With the exception of much of the park work, for which nearly $105 million was approved, Bennett had some involvement with nearly all the city's public works projects. By 1933, the Chicago Plan Commission could claim responsibility for widening or opening 57 streets. Between 1909 and 1930, the city had built 38 bridges and 17 viaducts.[42] In addition, Bennett represented the Chicago Plan Commission in negotiations for the locations of public buildings including Union Station, the Field Museum, the central Post Office, and the Cook County Criminal Court Building. Between 1921 and 1923, Bennett, along with his partners, William E. Parsons and Harry T. Frost, directed the large staff that prepared Chicago's first zoning ordinance. Although the Chicago Plan Commission had no direct connection with this work, Charles Wacker served as Secretary of the Zoning Commission, and Eugene S. Taylor, Plan Commission Manager, also became the Executive Secretary of the Zoning Commission.[43] Bennett's position led to other public works projects as well. For the South Park District, he designed the landscaping and architectural embellishments of Grant Park (figs. 14, 15), completed between 1916 and 1930.

Fig. 14
Model (unlocated) of the colonnaded fountain for Grant Park designed by Edward H. Bennett, 1915 (demolished). Sited on Randolph Street just west of the Illinois Central railroad tracks, it was 100 feet long with columns 24 feet high.

As a center piece for the formal lakefront park, he created Buckingham Fountain (figs. 16, 17; see cat. nos. 28, 29), which was dedicated in 1927. Because Kate S. Buckingham had commissioned this memorial to her late brother Clarence directly from the architect, Bennett's firm was able to design and supervise at least one public improvement from start to finish.[44]

At the suggestion of Plan Commission chairman James Simpson, the Executive Committee voted to abolish the consultant's position on August 5, 1930. Thus ended Bennett's role as the official upholder of Burnham's vision of the new Chicago. Appointment to an ineffectual Architect's Advisory Committee was little compensation.[45] Bennett's dismissal was never explained, but the reasons are easily surmised. On one hand, the city's worsening financial condition led the commission to cut its staff and forego recommendation of new public works. On the other, it is quite clear that Bennett felt that the Plan Commission, no longer controlled by his friends Wacker, Butler, and Moody, had abandoned fundamental elements of the Burnham Plan. Simpson and the other new leaders listened more and more to engineer Hugh E. Young and less to architect Bennett. In March 1930, they had approved Young's revised plans for the Outer Drive Bridge. For the Beaux-Arts classicism of the 1927 scheme, designed to harmonize with earlier improvements, he substituted a "modernistic style," which he claimed was "better and more suitable for the purpose."[46] Worse still was the Commission's endorsement of Young's idea to replace the (proposed) depressed Congress Street superhighway—the Burnham

Fig. 15
Construction of cast concrete balustrades, rostral columns, and other elements of the terraces in Grant Park, west of the Illinois Central railroad tracks, 1916.

Fig. 16
Buckingham Fountain, Grant Park, in a 1927 photograph, the year it was completed.

Fig. 17
Marcel Loyau (1895-1936), sculptor of the sea horses at Buckingham Fountain, in his Paris studio, c. 1927.

Plan axis—with an elevated highway along Monroe Street. Bennett, who had worked since 1927 on Congress Street plans, was outraged, and so were a number of west side groups. With the backing of the Affiliated Civic Associations, his firm produced studies to refute the Chicago Plan Commission (see cat. no. 9). In *The Axis of Chicago*, Bennett argued that shifting the axis was not only more costly, but that it also contradicted years of work to create two quadrangles of widened arterial streets around the retail and financial district to the north and the wholesale and warehouse district to the south—namely, Michigan Avenue, Wacker Drive, Market Street (now also Wacker Drive), Roosevelt Road, and Congress Street down the middle (fig. 18).[47] Young's scheme also abandoned another key element of the Burnham Plan that Bennett had defended for years—the civic center flanking Congress Street west of the river at Halsted Street. In approving the Monroe Street axis, the commission gave tacit approval to the Treasury Department's decision to switch sites for the new Post Office. This building on a two-block site, already purchased, between Harrison, Polk, Clinton, and Canal Streets, was to have been one of the first in the civic center, along with "Chicago Hall," an exposition and sports complex for which bonds had been approved in June 1927 (see cat. nos. 19, 20). The present Post Office building (fig. 19), designed by Graham, Anderson, Probst and White, also successors of Burnham, now sits between Van Buren, Harrison, and Canal Streets and the river, straddling Congress Street which runs through it. When plans for the building were revealed, Bennett labelled it "Ernest Graham's insult to Congress Street."[48] Even though his official connection with Chicago public improvements had ended, Bennett continued to follow this course, speaking out, for example, when the Congress expressway question came up again in the mid-1930s and making one of many proposals for railway consolidation in the late 1930s (see cat. no. 21). Meanwhile, he and his partners were busy with other commissions.

Fig. 18
Photomontage from January 1928 published in
The Axis of Chicago (1929).

Fig. 19
Aerial view, c. 1940, of the Congress Street area, showing the General Post Office (1939) designed by Graham, Anderson, Probst and White, before the construction of the Eisenhower Expressway. (Post Office, upper right.)

Many of Bennett's city plans, especially those completed before the First World War, resemble the Chicago Plan very closely. He recommended web-shaped networks of arterial streets and symmetrical civic centers, as well as practical improvements like railway consolidation. When possible, there were beautiful renderings by Jules Guérin or other artists illustrating proposed improvements. Even the layout and style of the published plan report for Minneapolis very closely resembles the prototype. This was not, however, slavish imitation, since the Chicago Plan and the Commission's promotion of it represented the state of the art of city planning for nearly a decade, and Bennett was hired by civic groups which desired a repeat performance by Burnham's protégé. The Chicago Plan remained the model of success among civic leaders, even while other city planners recognized its limitations.

Through 1915, Bennett made five comprehensive city plans, the ground plan for a world's fair, and several smaller urban design projects. The years immediately following the completion of the Chicago Plan must have been an exhilarating time. In September and October 1909, representatives from Detroit[49] and Portland, Oregon,[50] first contacted Burnham about plans for their cities. Bennett departed for a vacation to Europe and Egypt and, shortly after his return in February 1910, came commissions for the Minneapolis city plan,[51] the ground plan of the Panama-Pacific International Exposition in San Francisco (1915),[52] and a riverfront improvement scheme for Cedar Rapids.[53] In 1912, before these projects were completed, commissions for city plans were received from Brooklyn[54] and Ottawa.[55] Pittsburgh ordered a park plan in 1914.[56] Despite differences of scale and topography, these schemes all reveal Bennett's consistent approach to city planning, the same that guided his work in Chicago.

Bennett was hired as a planning consultant in each of these cities, yet in none of them did he personally execute any of the buildings, bridges, or parks he designed. Only in San Francisco, where the exhibition buildings were designed by others, was a plan carried out in entirety (see cat. no. 34). Even here, once the fair was over, the grounds were almost completely cleared for residential subdivision. These events typify the fate of plans of this era; the Chicago experience proved atypical. In only three cities—Detroit, Ottawa, and Cedar Rapids (see cat. no. 17)—did the plan sponsors have government backing. In Portland (figs. 20, 21), Minneapolis (see cat. nos. 23, 30), Brooklyn, and Pittsburgh, where voluntary organizations of civic leaders hired Bennett, virtually nothing in these cities was built according to his plans. Implementation could never be guaranteed. Success depended not only on the reasonableness of the plan, but also upon local politics and economic conditions, circumstances over which a consulting architect and planner from Chicago had no control. In general, it appears that Bennett's plans, like those of his fellow practitioners, had the best chance to guide development in cities with a strong support for planning where the new schemes incorporated and embellished the existing structure of the city and pre-existing ideas for public improvements.

The five comprehensive plans share a number of common elements with the plan of Chicago. Wherever possible, Bennett recommended opening and widening streets in order to create a symmetrical network of diagonal and circumferential boulevards that would ease traffic circulation and create an orderly and hierarchical urban structure. At the foci of these networks were to be civic centers. In Ottawa, the existing Parliament Buildings formed the nucleus of a proposed new government center. In Brooklyn, a civic center was to be developed around the Borough Hall in conjunction with the realignment of streets leading from the Brooklyn Bridge. In Minneapolis, a grand complex of public buildings was proposed around the intersection of two new cross axes which were to shift development away from the existing center. Neither the civic center nor the Sixth Avenue (Portland Avenue) axis was ever built. In

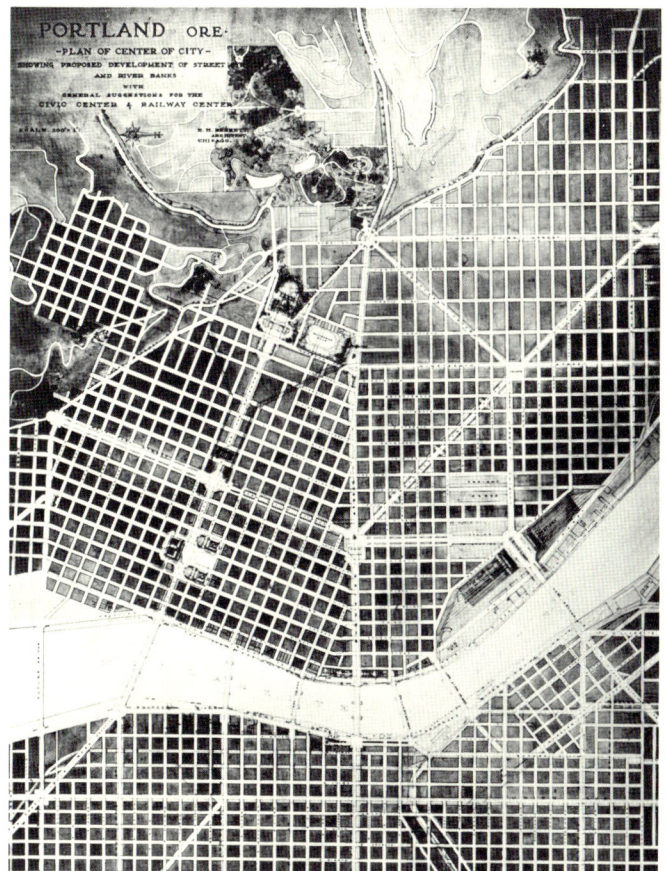

Fig. 20
Edward H. Bennett, *Plan of the Center of Portland, Oregon* (unlocated), 1912.

Fig. 21
General View of Portland toward the Willamette River (unlocated), rendered by Jules Guérin, c. 1912.

contrast, the Center of Arts and Letters that Bennett designed for Detroit's City Plan and Improvement Commission provided the location for Cass Gilbert's Public Library (1921) and Paul Cret's Institute of Arts (1927). In each of these plans, park systems received considerable attention, although some cities, such as Minneapolis, Brooklyn, and Portland, already possessed fine parks. Bennett also advocated neighborhood recreation centers, similar to the small playground parks in Chicago he had helped to design. Like Chicago, each of the cities in which Bennett worked during these years was sited on a river, with the exception of San Francisco, which is a peninsula surrounded by the ocean and a bay. Every plan displays a great sensitivity to the development of the waterfront. The plans for Minneapolis and Cedar Rapids are outstanding in this respect. Riverfronts were to be reclaimed from railroads and industries wherever possible and to be lined with embankments modeled on those of London, Paris, and other European capitals. Drawing on his concurrent work in Chicago, Bennett also proposed elegant bridges. In Cedar Rapids, his recommendations to the Riverfront Improvement Committee for the treatment of the banks of the Red Cedar River, for new bridges, and for the location of public buildings on the river island were largely executed. In Pittsburgh, however, where his work was sponsored by the Municipal Art Commission, Bennett's design for a formally landscaped park on the Point at the confluence of the Allegheny and Monongahela Rivers found little public support in 1914. As with a number of recommendations of this era, however, future generations vindicated the city beautifiers. Pittsburgh's Point State Park was authorized by the governor in 1945 and completed in the early 1970s.

Bennett's career had begun auspiciously, but beginning in 1915, a decline in new commissions forced a reduction in staff and wages in the office. No doubt the outbreak of the World War had some effect, but it is also probably true that the Burnham aura had faded. Bennett would now have to build a reputation on his own and forge new connections with potential clients. The years 1915 through 1919 were occupied with only ten commissions in addition to Chicago Plan work: two family projects and plans for two small Illinois towns—Elgin and Winnetka—a small Wisconsin college, three army cantonments, and a civic center in Denver. But the picture did improve. The 1920s witnessed many commissions from wealthy private patrons and from a number of city planning commissions around the country. Bennett, Parsons and Frost flourished as national economic conditions improved and as city planning became an increasingly accepted function of urban government.

Social connections have always been important for furthering an architect's career, and Bennett certainly profited from his. He settled in Lake Forest in about 1906; acquaintanceships from this wealthy North Shore community would lead to important work. His first Lake Forest residence was the Onwentsia Club, founded in 1896 and located on the former estate of architect Henry Ives Cobb.[57] Here, while watching a polo match, Bennett may have met Cyrus and Harold McCormick, Charles Dewey, or the Alexander McKinlocks, all of whom would provide commissions.[58] Perhaps here, too, he met Miss Catherine Jones, his future wife, whose parents, the David B. Joneses, lived in "Pembroke Hall" on Green Bay Road, an estate also designed by Cobb.[59] After their marriage in 1913, Catherine Bennett's bachelor uncle, Thomas D. Jones, gave the couple funds to build a large house on a corner of the Green Bay Road property. Much of Bennett's time during 1915 and 1916 was occupied with planning and supervising the construction of "Bagatelle" (fig. 22), designed in the style of an 18th-century French country house with a small but elegant garden to match.[60] At the same time, he participated in the design of the Lake Forest Market Square by Howard Van Doren Shaw, another prominent local architect. Bennett's father-in-law and Cyrus McCormick were among the original trustees of the development.[61] He designed also for Mr. David Jones an extensive landscape setting for a winter home in Montecito, California, near Santa Barbara, a favored resort of wealthy Lake Forest residents, including the Armours and Cudahys. The house at "Pepper Hill" was the work of David Adler, the architect of many grand Lake Forest houses. It resembled a 16th-century Italian villa, and the formal gardens by Bennett harmonized with the house and the spectacular hilltop setting.[62] Except for several subdivisions, these commissions were Bennett's only domestic work.

In sharp contrast to the elegant and comfortable environments of Montecito and Lake Forest were the three cantonments planned for the Army Quartermaster Corps in 1917 and 1918. With the advice of Frederick Law Olmsted, Jr., founder of the American City Planning Institute, the Army utilized the principles and methods of the new profession in building army camps and workers' housing. Camp Grant, south of Rockford, Illinois, the first of Bennett's cantonments, was laid out along several skewed axes between a rail line and the Rock River. Harry Frost supervised construction of this camp for over 40,000 troops and of Camp Las Casas in Puerto Rico. Camp Knox, 30 miles southeast of Knoxville, Kentucky, was begun under William Parsons' supervision, but work was halted with the signing of the armistice.[63]

The Denver civic center (cat. no. 24), along with those in San Francisco and Cleveland, is one of very few proposed civic centers to be built, even in part.[64] As in Chicago, civic improvement in Denver found wholehearted support in City Hall. Here, the key figure was "Boss" Robert Speer, a mayor reviled by reformers but devoted to the City Beautiful. With his encouragement, plans to

Fig. 22
The garden facade of "Bagatelle," Edward H. Bennett's house in Lake Forest, 1915-1916. Photo: Joan Draper.

29

embellish the grounds around the state capitol with landscaping and new public buildings had been made by well-known artists and planners, including Charles Mulford Robinson (1906), Frederick MacMonnies (1907), and Frederick Law Olmsted, Jr., and Arnold Brunner (1912). Although some land had been bought and cleared and a few pieces of sculpture donated, little progress was made until Speer's re-election in 1916. One of his first acts upon taking office was to call in Bennett. Existing plans called for the axial development of the grounds between the capitol and a proposed city-county building; these were enlarged and revised to strengthen a cross-axis between two memorials. The Colonnade of Civic Benefactors and Outdoor Theater was designed by local architects Moreau and Norton, with Bennett's advice forced upon them by the mayor. The Voorhies Monument, another curved colonnade across the axis, is the work of Fisher and Fisher, who were also advised by Bennett.[65] The design of these landscape elements in Denver resembles the western portions of Grant Park along Michigan Avenue, which had recently been completed.

During the 1920s, the office received calls for seven more civic centers. Both Parsons and Frost, and for a short time, Cyrus Thomas, became Bennett's partners during this prosperous period. Between 1919 and 1929, the firm made ten more comprehensive city plans and continued to produce subdivision and landscape plans as well. But its repertory was expanding. Six zoning ordinances, including one for Chicago, were produced. Perhaps Bennett's most significant work of the decade was one of six preliminary reports for the Regional Plan of New York and Environs, a landmark document in the history of American city planning.

By the mid-1920s, Bennett, Parsons and Frost had become one of the 23 professional planning firms in the country offering consultative services. The number of offices kept pace with the volume of work. In 1923, only 250 cities had made comprehensive plans and only slightly more than 100 had adopted zoning ordinances. By 1929, there were 650 plans and 754 zoning ordinances. Nevertheless, most cities still did not employ a planner continuously as Chicago did, although they were more likely to engage a technical staff to collect data and execute recommendations in their consultant's reports. Smaller cities were now as likely as large metropolises to plan for the future; about three-quarters of the reports published between 1920 and 1926 were for cities under 100,000.[66] The Bennett firm's work in the 1920s reflects this pattern. St. Paul and Buffalo requested their services, but so did a number of smaller municipalities in the Chicago region and the Midwest, including Gary, Fort Wayne, Joliet, Highland Park, and Lake Forest (figs. 23, 24). Characteristically, nearly three-quarters of their urban work, including plans, zoning ordinances, and public building plans, came from official city planning agencies, rather than from organizations of businessmen.

Throughout the country the nature of planning work was changing. Boosterish rhetoric and utopian visions of magnificent boulevards and public buildings gave way to more cautious, technical language backed by mountains of statistics and illustrated with traffic flow diagrams and land use maps. The change, usually described as the transition from City Beautiful to City Functional, reflected both the growing professionalization of planning and the challenge presented by the automobile.[67] The Bennett and Parsons plan for the St. Paul City Planning Board of 1922 is strikingly different from the 1917 Minneapolis Plan. Its co-author, George H. Herrold, was the city engineer, not another planner. The St. Paul report is paperbound and has no color renderings. Its major elements are an historical overview of local planning, a survey of existing conditions, a preliminary plan mostly devoted to street widenings, a detailed analysis of traffic in the central business district, a discussion of sidewalks and business development, a report by Chicago consultants on railroads, a zoning

Fig. 23
Plans for Elgin (1917), Winnetka (1921), Joliet (1921), and St. Paul (1922).

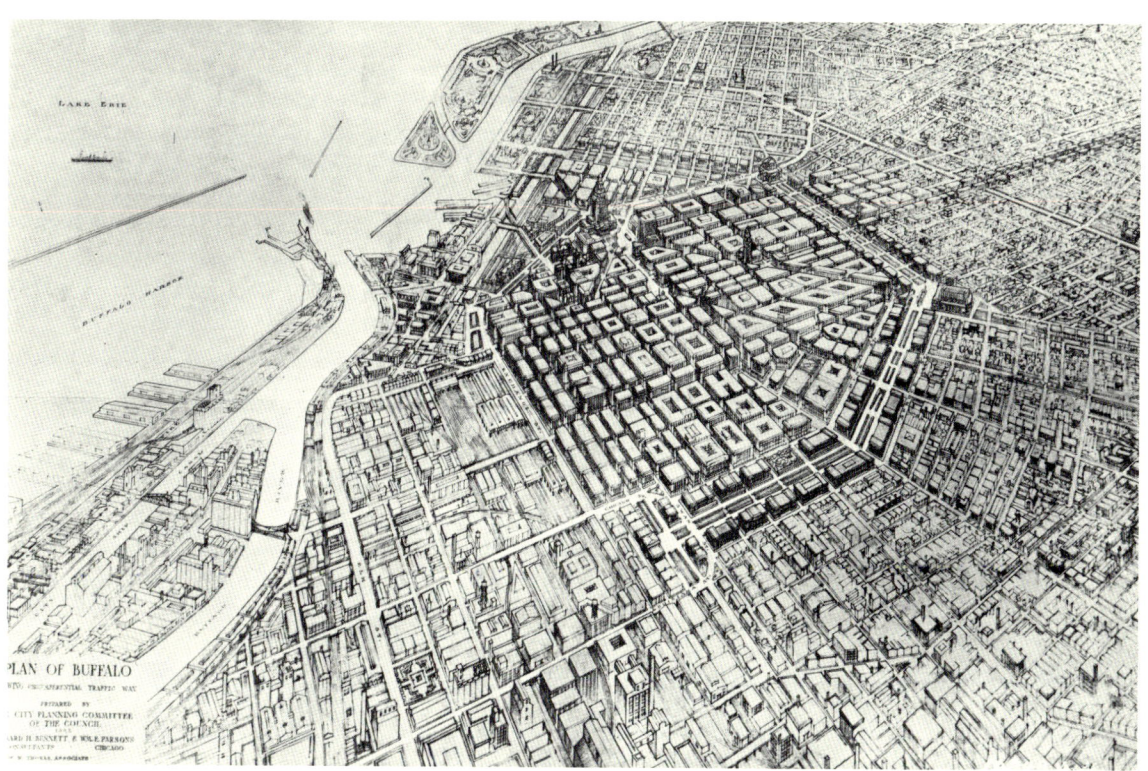

Fig. 24
Bennett and Parsons with Thomas and Frost, Associates, *Plan of Buffalo Showing Circumferential Traffic Way* (unlocated), 1922.

study and plan, and recommendations for enlarging the park system. The civic center proposal is modest, here defended with statistics on floor space rather than with appeals to civic patriotism, and illustrated with one, simple line drawing. The first improvements carried out in accord with this plan and later designs by Bennett were street widenings, among them the rebuilding of Third Street (now Kellogg Boulevard) along the river to create a double-decked roadway similar to Chicago's Wacker Drive.[68] Equally practical and conservative is Bennett's plan for Winnetka, begun in 1917, but not completed and published until 1921. Here he aimed to preserve the country-like setting of this attractive North Shore suburb. Bennett recommended diverting automobile and truck traffic away from the lakeshore and off residential streets to designated highways, passing a zoning ordinance to keep industry and commerce out of residential areas, depressing the tracks of the commuter rail line through Winnetka, locating new parks and school sites for future development, and creating a village center around the railway station. Much of the plan was executed over the years.[69]

As a resident of the area, Bennett's concern for preserving the exclusive and tranquil character of the North Shore naturally continued. In 1923, his firm completed a study for a zoning ordinance for Lake Forest, and in 1929, a planning report. Persistent traffic problems led the North Shore Property Owners Association to commission a North Shore Plan in 1937. Like the Winnetka plan, it recommended the elimination of grade crossings by depressing tracks and the rerouting of traffic from Sheridan Road along the lakeshore to Green Bay and Glencoe Roads to the west.[70] All of these suggestions accorded with the principles of the Chicago Regional Planning Association. This organization, founded in 1923, encouraged local authorities to make their own plans, while it worked to coordinate parks, highways, and other regional concerns.[71]

Although Bennett had no official role in the Chicago association, he was among the planning experts who contributed to the New York Regional Plan. This landmark document, published in eight survey volumes and two plan volumes between 1927 and 1931,[72] represented the most extensive effort to coordinate development in a metropolitan area yet attempted in the United States. Its inspiration was the explicitly regional perspective of the Chicago Plan of 1909. The leader of the movement in New York, Charles D. Norton, had been one of the men most active in the Chicago Plan. After serving as Assistant Secretary of the Treasury, he moved to New York. In 1914, Norton was appointed to the City Planning Advisory Committee and soon thereafter had outlined an ambitious program for his adopted city, stating, "Let some Daniel H. Burnham do for this immense community what Burnham did for Chicago and its environs."[73] To most of the men whom Norton tried to interest in his proposal, a New York regional plan seemed impossibly ambitious. But in 1920, he was able to convince his fellow trustees of the Russell Sage Foundation, which had supported other planning activities, to underwrite this effort. Norton consulted expert advisors from New York and elsewhere, notables in business, politics, and the professions. These men included Frederick Law Olmsted, Jr.,; Edward Bassett, a lawyer and the "father" of zoning; Frederic A. Delano, a railroad executive and former member of the Chicago Plan team; Charles Moore, author of the Chicago Plan and now Chairman of the Commission of Fine Arts in Washington; Thomas Adams, first president of the Town Planning Institute of Great Britain and lecturer at M.I.T.; and his good friend Edward H. Bennett.

Following advice from Delano and Adams, Norton modified his initial proposal to duplicate the Chicago experience. These men had cautioned him against identifying the plan with one strong Burnham-like personality. Instead, groups of specialists began the work in 1922, directed by a committee which

Norton chaired. The staff consisted of men expert in different fields, including Nelson P. Lewis, recently retired Chief Engineer of New York; Shelby Harrison, a social worker and member of the Sage Foundation staff; and Bassett. Consultants in various fields also contributed. In December 1922, six leaders in city planning were chosen to study land use, industrial and commercial development, transportation systems, subdivision controls, and open space in each of six sectors of the New York region. These men were Harland Bartholomew, George B. Ford, and John Nolen, as well as Adams, Olmsted, and Bennett. They completed preliminary written reports and maps which indicated problems and possible solutions. Adams synthesized these to produce a Draft Report of the Advisory Planning Group, dated November 12, 1923. Although never published, this report strongly influenced the final plan as it was developed under Delano and Adams, who assumed the project's direction after Norton's death in 1923.[74]

Again, when his role in the Regional Plan is compared to that of his colleagues, Bennett does not appear to have been a leader or pioneer. Planning historian David A. Johnson considers Bennett's contribution the weakest of the six consultants, even though Bennett's report on Sector VI (Staten Island and southern New Jersey) reveals how far his thinking had advanced beyond the overly formal and aesthetically determined plans of the pre-war period.[75] All the experts involved in the Regional Plan of New York and its Environs, however, shared some of the shortcomings of the planning profession in the 1920s. As critic Lewis Mumford pointed out, they were too cautious and too technically oriented. The New York plan failed to deal adequately with housing problems and to suggest how the growth of the region could be controlled or directed. In their concentration on efficient automobile transportation, the planners revealed a suburban, upper-middle-class bias.[76]

Although his firm specialized in the planning profession's more technical aspects, Bennett never forsook the ideals of the City Beautiful Movement. In addition to zoning and traffic studies, a number of commissions after 1919 gave him the opportunity to design riverfront esplanades, pleasant suburban and resort neighborhoods, parks, fountains, monuments, and seven groupings of public buildings. Many of these commissions came from wealthy clients; Chicago's Buckingham Fountain, as we have seen, memorializes one of the city's art patrons, Clarence Buckingham, and was the gift of his sister Kate. Contributions for the Pasteur Memorial, now opposite Cook County Hospital, came from many prominent Chicagoans. The Phipps family, whose fortune came from U.S. Steel, requested designs for its properties in Palm Beach, Florida; Barnegat Beach, New Jersey; and on Sutton Place in New York. Vincent Astor needed a subdivision plan for Port Washington, Long Island. The grounds of Lake Forest's Knollwood Country Club follow a landscape plan by Bennett. And an old Lake Forest friend, Marion McKinlock, commissioned a city plan for Palm Beach, that lush, tropical paradise resort of the rich, where she served as president of the garden club.[77] But municipal commissions for beautification were not altogether lacking either. Unfortunately, but not surprisingly, only two of these designs from the 1920s were executed: a riverfront park in Tiffin, Ohio,[78] and the Pasadena, California, civic center (cat. no. 25).[79]

A comparison of this latter scheme of 1923 with earlier civic center projects for San Francisco, Chicago, and Minneapolis is revealing. Instead of cutting new diagonal streets and anticipating a dramatic expansion of the central business district, the Pasadena plan accommodates itself to existing conditions. The civic center, one part of a larger general plan, is located about two intersecting streets, one parallel to the main commercial avenue, which were extended and widened to create appropriate sites for public buildings. Its location and configuration resulted as much from the need to improve traffic circulation as to position the proposed city hall, library, and civic auditorium at the ends of the two axes. To the west of city hall, along the Holly Street axis, Bennett and his associate, French landscape architect Jacques H. Lambert, also designed a Center of Arts in Carmelita Park (cat. no. 31). This is now the site of the Norton Simon Museum of Art (formerly Pasadena Art Museum), but the exotic landscaping planned to surround the proposed museum was never completed. The buildings in the civic center, however, did materialize. The domed city hall, designed by Bakewell and Brown of San Francisco, old friends of Bennett's from Paris days, was constructed between 1925 and 1927. The library, by Myron Hunt, formerly of Chicago, was constructed simultaneously, and the civic auditorium at the opposite end of the cross axis was completed in 1932. Other public and semi-public buildings were added over the years. Only a recent commercial structure blocking the view down the axis to the auditorium mars the cohesiveness of this attractive ensemble.

The depression virtually ended this sort of work for Bennett, Parsons and Frost, as it did for countless other architects and planners. No new commissions for civic centers, urban plans, or zoning studies came to the office in the 1930s. Even the Chicago Plan work had ended. Fortunately, the firm's prestige had attracted several jobs of a different sort—all monumental or ornamental in character—that did get built during these hard times. In 1928, the George Rogers Clark Sesquicentennial Commission hired William Parsons to act as its architectural advisor for the competition for the design of the memorial in Vincennes, Indiana. With federal, state, and city funding, the round doric temple by Frederick Hirons of New York, the landscaping, and the Lincoln Memorial Bridge over the Wabash River by Parsons were completed in 1935.[80] New Orleans commissioned a plan for enlarging its City Park in 1933, and with W.P.A. funds this was completed several years later.[81] Bennett was primarily occupied with two special jobs that must have seemed a satisfying finale to his career. In 1927, he became Chairman of the Board of Architects in charge of designing the Federal Triangle, a new departmental complex in Washington, D.C. The next year, he was selected as one of the designers of the projected 1933 world's fair in Chicago. These commissions more closely resembled his first monumental planning work at the Ecole des Beaux-Arts or for West Point than anything he had done since. They kept the office busy until the late 1930s, by which time its members had more or less retired from active practice.

When Chicago's second world's fair was conceived in the '20s by some of the city's richest men, it seemed only natural to celebrate its 100th birthday with a rousing celebration of progress in science. The theme of the Century of Progress Exposition, as it ultimately came to be known, would be expressed architecturally. While money was raised from magnates like Wrigley and McCormick, Chairman Rufus Dawes sought the architects. He first turned to Raymond Hood, designer of Chicago's Tribune Tower and other skyscrapers in his home city of New York, and to Paul Cret, a Philadelphia architect known for his public buildings. These two men recommended three others with excellent reputations and the ability to cooperate. They were Harvey Wiley Corbett and Ralph Walker of New York and Arthur Brown, Jr., of San Francisco. Local men of equal eminence were then named: John Holabird, Hubert Burnham, and Edward Bennett. This selection was an interesting mixture of conservative, Beaux-Arts-trained men and those less historically minded with more experience in the realm of commercial architecture. Of the Chicagoans, Holabird belonged in the latter category. Burnham and Bennett were, appropriately, the son and protégé of the guiding spirit behind the 1893 World's Fair. Daniel H. Burnham, Jr., was later appointed Director of Works. Clarence Farrier, manager of the Bennett office, became Assistant Director, and Louis Skidmore, just out of M.I.T., was made Chief of Design. Others were added; this was not to be a team where one dominant personality and aesthetics ruled, at least during the initial phases of the design process.[82]

Bennett felt out of sympathy with the ultimate scheme developed for the exposition grounds, which were located on two bands of filled land defining a lagoon between 12th and 39th Streets. Although he had been appointed in 1928 to make the general plan, it was decided that the team would produce it together. Each of the eight principal designers submitted preliminary drawings (fig. 25). These were then combined into an "accepted *parti*" in January 1929. These preliminary schemes shared common features. They emphasized verticality and were organized symmetrically about two cross axes, one parallel to the shore and the other at 23rd Street. In each, circulation was handled by an upper level of ramps, so that visitors would move down through the exhibition halls.[83] But the combined scheme was rejected as impractical and old-fashioned. The awkward site could not be made symmetrical without extensive

Fig. 25
Bennett, Parsons and Frost with J. H. Lambert, preliminary study (unlocated) from 1929 for the 1933 Century of Progress Exposition.

filling operations. A new solution was found when Raymond Hood arrived at a May 1929 meeting with an asymmetrical plan. When revised by Cret, it was accepted and became the basis of the final scheme (fig. 26). After the vote, however, Bennett complained in his diary that "picturesqueness and individuality won 5-3." He later wrote, "my ultimate feeling is that it is an ignoble plan, but would be accepted by the public."[84] The defenders of the scheme praised its flexibility, which, in fact, became an important factor when the stock market crash forced a reduction in scale and shuffling of tenants in the proposed buildings. Furthermore, soil conditions were poor and the ground may never have supported the huge symmetrical towers of the earlier proposals.

Bennett is credited with the design and co-design of six major structures in the exposition: the Administration Building (with Burnham and Holabird), the Agriculture Building (with Brown), the Dairy Building (with Brown), the Federal

Fig. 26
Aerial view of the Century of Progress Exposition, 1933.

Building (alone) (cat. no. 33), the Hall of States (with Brown), and the Travel and Transport Building (with Burnham and Holabird). But his diaries and the designs themselves suggest that the government buildings and the Administration Building received his closest attention. Both are symmetrical and hierarchically composed, revealing, at least in their massing, a classically trained hand. In their brilliant coloration and technical innovation, all the exposition buildings represented a departure from tradition. The extent of Bennett's involvement with the structural design and detailing, however, is not clear. He oversaw the color studies of the Federal Building, which had blue walls, a gold dome, and three 150-foot tall gold and white pylons surrounding it. But the use of lightweight metal frameworks and pre-manufactured decking and wall panels must be attributed to others. These were experimental structures, making use of new materials and construction techniques developed by the building industry. The Travel and Transport Building's main enclosure was the first suspended structure in the country.[85] It is doubtful whether this or other innovations can be attributed to Bennett.

While at work on the Chicago exposition, Bennett and his partners were involved in a larger and probably more congenial project, the success of which depended upon the coordinated efforts of seven like-minded architects and seven huge buildings designed in the grand classical tradition. The Public Buildings Act of 1926 authorized a vast federal program in Washington, D.C., under the direction of a Board of Architects (fig. 27) appointed the following year. Bennett served as the board's chairman until 1937, and his job included coordinating the design of the Federal Triangle (fig. 28), a complex of new offices between the Capitol and the White House. Lodged in these buildings were the Departments of Commerce, Labor, and Justice, the Post Office, the Interstate Commerce Commission, the Internal Revenue Service, the Federal Trade Commission, and the National Archives. The board also consulted about the siting of other proposed structures, including the Supreme Court, in the monumental core of the capital. Each member was allotted the design of one Triangle building. To Bennett, Parsons and Frost came the commission for the Apex Building

Fig. 27
Board of Architects for the Federal Triangle, Washington, D.C. From left to right: John Russell Pope, Clarence Zantzinger, Louis A. Simon, Edward H. Bennett, Arthur Brown, Jr., and William A. Delano.

Fig. 28
Bird's-eye view drawing of the Federal Triangle plan from *Journal of the American Institute of Architects*, XVI (1928).

Fig. 29
Aerial view of Washington, D.C., looking east toward the Capitol, including the Apex Building and the landscaping seen in Fig. 32. Under construction at the middle left border is the National Gallery of Art designed by John Russell Pope, finished c. 1941.

Fig. 30
Bennett, Parsons and Frost, the Apex Building at the tip of the Federal Triangle at 6th Street looking west. This photograph, taken soon after the Apex Building was completed in 1938, shows the building as substantially designed by Bennett in 1931.

Fig. 31
Bennett, Parsons and Frost, drawing (unlocated) of the elevation of the Botanic Gardens Conservatory in Washington, D.C., 1931-33.

Fig. 32
Bennett, Parsons and Frost, bird's-eye view drawing (unlocated) of the proposed landscaping for the Capitol Grounds Extension between the Capitol, Union Station, and Louisiana and Delaware Avenues, c. 1933.

(figs. 29, 30, cat. no. 26), which houses the Federal Trade Commission. In addition, the firm designed the new Botanic Gardens Conservatory (fig. 31) facing the mall at the foot of Capitol Hill and all the landscaping for both the Triangle and the newly cleared area lying between the Capitol, Union Station, and Louisiana and Delaware Avenues (fig. 32).

Bennett was a natural choice for the chairmanship of the board. His skills in dealing with complex architectural and planning problems that needed the approval of powerful politicians and several review commissions were well known to the men who selected him. He was first contacted about the job in April 1925 by Charles S. Dewey, Assistant Secretary of the Treasury and former Lake Forest resident and vice-president of the Northern Trust Company in Chicago. Dewey recommended Bennett to Secretary of the Treasury Andrew Mellon, under whose jurisdiction fell the design and construction of all federal buildings. In September 1926, Bennett was appointed the Secretary's personal architectural consultant before the Board of Architects was named. Two other old friends directed commissions that were to play an important role in shaping the Triangle. Frederic Delano, a leader in both the Chicago Plan and the New York Regional Plan, now headed the newly created National Capital Park and Planning Commission. Chairing the Commission of Fine Arts was Charles Moore, likewise a major participant in both those earlier undertakings. The architects selected to make up the board were all skilled classicists with impressive lists of buildings to their credit. Louis A. Simon, Supervising Architect of the Treasury, was naturally a member of the group. From New York came John Russell Pope, architect of the Lincoln Memorial; William A. Delano of Delano and Aldrich; and Louis Ayers of York and Sawyer. Arthur Brown, Jr., of San Francisco and Milton Medary of the Philadelphia firm Zantzinger, Borie and Medary completed the team. The friendships and similar tastes of these men by no means precluded conflicts over elements of the Triangle complex, but never was there any question about the underlying principles that guided its design.[86]

The new additions to monumental Washington completed important segments of the McMillan Commission Plan of 1901-02. Daniel Burnham, Charles McKim, Frederick Law Olmsted, Jr., and Augustus St. Gaudens, all veterans of the Chicago World's Fair, had been appointed by the Senate to re-plan the Mall and park system in the federal district in order to reinstate Pierre L'Enfant's 18th-century plan. The Triangle and formal landscaping around the Capitol had been defined by their drawings and documents. It was now up to Burnham's successor to execute these important elements, which are crucial to the creation of the sense of grandeur and to the definition of the Mall and the Capitol approach from the north. Bennett began general site plans and facade studies immediately in 1926, willingly following directives from Secretary Mellon and President Hoover to avoid modern "blunt" architecture and to work within the vocabulary of "the eighteenth century classic." In letters and memos, frequent references were made to French precedents. "While having each a separate treatment," advised Mellon, the buildings "shall be of harmonious design grouped around two large interior courts or plazas somewhat after the arrangement of the Louvre."[87] In general, this ideal was followed, although the buildings as designed depend not on the Louvre for their inspiration but on the work of Ange Jacques Gabriel and other neoclassicists. All are clad in limestone and respect the same cornice and basement lines. Particular attention was also paid to the interconnectedness of the separate buildings of the Triangle. Early criticism of Bennett's first scheme by the press and the Fine Arts Commission led to much closer coordination of all the structures by the architects later appointed to design them. The board's correspondence and the minutes of the Fine Arts Commission reveal the lengthy process of design, criticism, and redesign which resulted in the final scheme of 1932. Sharp differences arose over several issues. The motif connecting the Great Court and the smaller circular court between the Post Office and I.R.S. Buildings along 12th Street was resolved contrary to the wishes of Bennett, who wanted a more dramatic treatment. The site of Pope's Archives Building and its relation to Bennett's neighboring Apex Building was disputed, as was this question of including a pool in the Great Court. The issues were ultimately settled, but not without occasionally calling upon political supporters to influence decisions. Later, Bennett, who won some battles and lost others, praised "the spirit of self-sacrifice shown by individual members of the Board."[88] Unfortunately, many of the much contested landscape features, which included kiosks, pylons, and lamp standards, were never executed. The Great Court became a parking lot, since the recommendation to build an underground parking garage here was not followed. Nor was the northwest corner of the block in which the court sits completed. Yet, the extension of the Capitol grounds and the new Botanic Gardens Conservatory (designed by Parsons) were carried out.[89]

The Apex Building, sitting at the eastern tip of the Triangle, as its name implies, was the last building completed and one of the simplest in detail. Bennett fought not only to have his designs approved, but also to keep the building itself a part of the ensemble. He began designs in January 1931; the following year, he found himself in conflict with Moore of the Fine Arts Commission and Ayres and Pope of the Board of Architects. They apparently objected to his treatment of the eastern portion of the building. The design was revised and finally approved in principle at a January 1934 joint meeting of the board and the two commissions. But another threat arose. A representative from New York, unaware of the Triangle plans, proposed a Jefferson Memorial on the site long designated for the Apex. With the aid of Delano, who took Bennett's case to his uncle, President Franklin Delano Roosevelt, both these issues were resolved. Final plans were approved in 1936, and the building was completed in 1938, although in a form stripped of much of the detail originally conceived by Bennett to harmonize with the more elaborate, earlier structures.[90] To modern eyes, however, the simplicity increases its power and helps this small building hold its own in such grand surroundings.

After completion of the Apex Building, the office had very little work, as Bennett, Parsons, and Frost intended to retire. William Parsons withdrew from the firm in 1938 to teach at Yale, his alma mater. He died the next year. Bennett and Frost maintained their partnership until the latter's death in 1944. The senior partner filled his days traveling between houses in Lake Forest, New Mexico, and North Carolina. He returned to his first love, painting in watercolors, and, until his death in 1954, frequently exhibited his paintings in Chicago.[91]

Clearly, Edward H. Bennett's career reflected changes in architecture and planning between 1900 and 1940, but his attitudes remained remarkably consistent, nonetheless. An architect trained in the Beaux-Arts tradition, he became a prominent member of the new and increasingly technical planning profession. Yet the two facets of his career—the aesthetic and the scientific—were never fully integrated into a single approach. While zoning and traffic studies issued forth from the office, mainly from the hands of assistants, Bennett frequently occupied himself at the drafting table or in the conference room with upholding the ideals of the City Beautiful Movement.

Bennett never deviated from the principles of his mentor, Daniel H. Burnham, even in the '20s and '30s as planners developed legal, statistical, and administrative techniques for coping with urban problems only partially envisioned in earlier decades. Like many who apprenticed under brilliant and charismatic men and who were fortunate to be at the forefront of developments in their fields, he did not push far beyond the territory so early surveyed. Instead, he consolidated the gains of the preceding generation. This conservatism was both a matter of personality and milieu. Although not born to wealth, Bennett adapted with ease to the style of life his marriage made possible. His friends, like his clients, were drawn from the business and social elite of Chicago and its suburbs. He appears to have been a gentleman of integrity, intelligence, and taste, but without the vision and ambition or the sense of alienation that drove some of his contemporaries to become pioneers or rebels. Nor was there much impetus to innovate or forsake the Beaux-Arts architect's approach to city planning. As this overview of his career has demonstrated, Bennett always found clients who valued his skills and shared his view of the city as a growing organism which only needed to be shaped by rational and, it seemed, well-defined principles. Those principles, as Burnham had set them out, derived not only from an understanding of functional relationships, but also from the need to express social and political ideals in physical form: "Make no little plans . . . a noble, logical diagram once recorded will never die . . . . Let your watchword be order and your beacon beauty."[92] For Bennett, as for his patrons across the country, Burnham's injunction still served. The buildings, bridges, fountains, monuments and parks Bennett designed, or whose shape and placement he influenced, are testaments to a view of city life which may seem outmoded and inappropriate today. Nevertheless, they have enhanced Chicago and other cities by both their utility and their beauty.

Abbreviations

AABN	*American Architect and Building News*
AIAJ	*American Institute of Architects Journal*
AIPJ	*American Institute of Planners Journal*
APAJ	*American Planning Association Journal*
Arch. Rec.	*Architectural Record*
ASPO	*American Society of Planning Officials*
CABN	*California Architect and Building News*
DHB	Daniel H. Burnham
EHB	Edward H. Bennett
HTF	Harry T. Frost
ISAMB	*Illinois Society of Architects Monthly Bulletin*
JSAH	*Journal of the Society of Architectural Historians*
RIBAJ	*Royal Institute of British Architects Journal*
WEP	William E. Parsons

Notes

1. See Bennett Family Tree, EHB Papers in possession of Edward H. Bennett, Jr.; The Society of Merchant Venturers, Merchant Venturers School, Analysis of Examinations by the Department of Science and Art in May 1887 and May 1888; "The Merchant Venturers Technical College," *The Gentleman's Journal* (Dec. 15, 1897), pp. 2739, 2742-43.

2. See F. S. Swales, "Master Draftsmen, XIV, Edward H. Bennett," *Pencil Points* VI (Aug. 1923), pp. 42-56. Published renderings by Bennett are "Building at Geary and Polk [San Francisco]," *CABN* XIII (July 1892), ill.; "The Wallace," *CABN* XIII (Oct. 1892), ill.; "Robert H. White Residence," *CABN* XIV (Nov. 1893), ill.

3. EHB to Phoebe Apperson Hearst, Jan. 7, 1900; Apr. 20, 1902; Sept. 24, 1904, Phoebe Apperson Hearst Correspondence and Papers, Bancroft Library, University of California, Berkeley; K. H. Cardwell, *Bernard Maybeck, Artisan, Architect, Artist* (Santa Barbara, 1977), pp. 38-39. Bennett's scholarship was not granted until December 1898.

4. On the importance of the Ecole des Beaux-Arts for Americans, see J. E. Draper, "The Ecole des Beaux-Arts and the Architectural Profession in the United States: The Case of John Galen Howard," in *The Architect. Chapters in the History of the Profession*, ed. Spiro Kostof (New York, 1977), pp. 209-37.

5. Swales (note 2), p. 43.

6. On Bennett's years in Paris and London, see his letters to Marion Polk, from January 1896 to July 2, 1899, in possession of Charles Polk, San Francisco.

7. "The Prizes and Studentships, 1902," *RIBAJ* IX (Jan. 25, 1902), p. 143. See also "The Prizes and Studentships, 1901," *RIBAJ* VII (Jan. 26, 1901), pp. 129-30; J. A. Gotch, "Review of Works Submitted for Prizes and Studentships," *RIBAJ* VIII (Mar. 9, 1901), p. 206.

8. EHB to Phoebe Apperson Hearst, April 20, 1902; Hearst Correspondence and Papers (note 3).

9. Staff List and Pay Ledger, George B. Post Papers, New York Historical Society. On Post's work see W. Weisman, "The Commercial Architecture of George B. Post," *JSAH* XXXI (Oct. 1972), pp. 176-203.

10. DHB to EHB, March 4 and 6, 1903; Peirce Anderson to EHB, March 5, 1903, Daniel H. Burnham Papers, Burnham Library, The Art Institute of Chicago; C. Moore, *Daniel H. Burnham, Architect, Planner of Cities*, 2 vols. (Boston and New York, 1921), I, p. 191.

11. Edward H. Bennett, typescript (about Daniel Burnham), n.d. [post-1912], EHB Papers, Burnham Library, The Art Institute of Chicago. The print is unidentified.

12. On Burnham's work in Washington, D.C., and Cleveland, see T. S. Hines, *Burnham of Chicago* (New York, 1974), pp. 139-75.

13. M. Schuyler, "The Architecture of West Point," *Arch. Rec.* XIV (Dec. 1903), p. 478; see also C. Field, "The City Planning of Daniel Hudson Burnham" (Ph.D. diss., Columbia University, 1974), p. 238.

14. DHB to Phelan, May 11, 1903, Burnham Papers.

15. DHB to Bishop Satterlee, June 25, 1906, quoted in Moore (note 10), II, p. 57.

16. See, for example, "Chicago Parks and Their Landscape Architecture." *Arch. Rec.* XXIV (July 1908), p. 19. On the small parks in general, see South Park Commissioners, *South Park Official Proceedings* VII (1904), p. 377; VIII (1905), p. 358; idem, *Report of the South Park Commissioners to the Board of County Commissioners of Cook County, December 1902-November 30, 1903* (Chicago, 1904), p. 10; idem, *Annual Report, South Park Commissioners. Fiscal Year 1904* (Chicago, 1905), pp. 6-9; Chicago Special Park Commission, *Report of the Special Park Commission to the City Council . . . of Chicago on the subject of a Metropolitan Park System,* comp. Dwight Heald Perkins (Chicago, 1904); Chicago Park District, *Historical Register of the Twenty Two Superseded Park Districts Compiled under the Supervision of the Division of the Secretary, Chicago Park District . . . By the Works Progress Administration,* ed. D. F. Breen (Chicago, 1941); Chicago Park District, Park Drawings; C. E. Rainwater, *The Play Movement in the United States* (Chicago, 1921), pp. 84-100; M. P. McCarthy, "Politics and the Parks. Chicago Businessmen and the Recreation Movement," *Journal of the Illinois State Historical Society* LXV (1972), pp. 158-72.

17. DHB to Phelan, November 20, 1905; DHB to William Greer Harrison, September 15, 1905, Burnham Papers.

18. DHB, *Report on a Plan for San Francisco* (San Francisco, 1905), p. 7.

19. For an account of Bennett's experiences in San Francisco, see EHB Diaries, May 11-Aug. 3, 1906, in the possession of Edward H. Bennett, Jr. See also J. E. Draper, "The San Francisco Civic Center: Architecture, Planning and Politics" (Ph.D. diss., University of California, Berkeley, 1979), pp. 90-106; Hines (note 12), pp. 174-96; J. Kahn, *Imperial San Francisco. Politics and Planning in an American City* (Lincoln, Neb., 1979).

20. See EHB Diaries, July 13-24, 1909, and October 11-12, 1911; Draper (note 19), pp. 125-73.

21. DHB to N. P. Avery, December 20, 1906, Burnham Papers.

22. DHB and EHB, *Plan of Chicago* (Chicago, 1909). The secondary literature on the plan is extensive. See especially R. P. Akeley, "Implementation of the 1909 Plan of Chicago: An Historical Account of Planning Salesmanship" (Master's Thesis, University of Tennessee, 1973); C. W. Condit, *Chicago 1910-29. Building, Planning, and Urban Technology* (Chicago and London, 1973), pp. 59-85; Hines (note 12), pp. 312-45; M. P. McCarthy, "Chicago Businessmen and the Burnham Plan," *Journal of the Illinois State Historical Society* LXIII (Autumn 1970), pp. 228-56; R. A. Walker, *The Planning Function in Urban Government*, 2nd ed. (Chicago, 1950), pp. 223-64; R. Bruegmann, S. Chappell, and J. Zukowsky, *The Plan of Chicago: 1909-1970* (Chicago, 1979).

23. Burnham employed the French architect Georges Fernand Janin. Bennett brought from France a 1909 Grand Prix *logiste,* Marcel Vilain. On the Bennett office staff, see Henri Maillard to EHB, October 18, 1911; Ben Holden to EHB, November 12 and 19, 1911, and April 4, 1912; J. P. Daubner to EHB, December 18, 1911, and April 29, 1912, EHB Papers. The EHB Diaries, 1906-12, contain frequent references to conferences with DHB and work on D. H. Burnham and Co. projects.

24. Parsons was born in Akron, Ohio, in 1872. He earned a B.A. from Yale University and an M.S. from Columbia University. In 1898, with a McKim Fellowship, he entered the Ecole des Beaux-Arts. He and Bennett probably knew each other, although they were in different ateliers and there is no record of their having met in Paris. Parsons left in 1900 without a diploma and went to work for John Galen Howard in New York. Howard soon moved to California. Bennett, writing from San Francisco to Burnham in 1905, recommended Parsons for the Philippines job, and he was subsequently recommended by Burnham to the Philippine commissioner. At the time, Parsons apparently had his own practice in New York. His work in Manila includes the Philippine General Hospital, Manila Hotel, Normal School, University Hall of the University of the Philippines, Central School, Y.M.C.A., Elks' Club, the Railway Station, and a fire station, in addition to a revision of Burnham's plan for the city. He also designed buildings in Baguio, La Laguna, Cebu, Capiz, Iloilo, Albay, Pampanga, Parlac, and elsewhere. Concerning the recommendations of Parsons for the Philippines job, see EHB to DHB, July 25, 1905; Peirce Anderson to WEP, September 9, 1905; DHB to W. Cameron Forbes, October 6, 1905, DHB Papers. On Parson's work, see WEP, "Burnham as a Pioneer in City Planning," *Arch. Rec.* XXXVII (July 1915), pp. 13-32; A. N. Rebori, "The Work of William E. Parsons in the Philippine Islands," *Arch. Rec.* XLI (Apr. 1917), pp. 305-24; (May 1917), pp. 424-34; T. S. Hines, "American Modernism in the Philippines: The Forgotten Architecture of William E. Parsons," *JSAH* XXII (Dec. 1973), pp. 316-26.

25. Harry T. Frost, born in England in 1886, attended Ohio State University and graduated from George Washington University in 1910. Before going to Chicago, he worked for the Supervising Architect of the Treasury in Washington, D.C. Frost died in 1944, at which time he and Bennett were still in partnership. Between 1922 and 1924, the firm was called Bennett, Parsons, Frost and Thomas. Cyrus Thomas, a graduate of the University of Pennsylvania (1917) and the Ecole des Beaux-Arts (1929?), worked for Cass Gilbert and Whitney Warren (New York), Mewes and Davis and Thomas W. Mawson (London), and Schmidt, Garden and Martin (Chicago), before joining the Bennett firm. See resumes: one attached to a letter from Bennett, Parsons, Frost and Thomas to Albert H. Hopkins, January 26, 1933; the other is "Personnel" (c. 1940); also see contracts, December 20, 1918; January 2, 1919; February 28 and April 1, 1922; May 1, 1929; June 1, 1938, EHB Papers.

26. Interview with Paul McCurry and Vincent Viscariello, October 1981. Both men graduated from Armour Institute in the 1920s, and Mr. Viscariello worked for Bennett. See also *ISAMB* I-VI (1916-22); Chicago Architectural Club, *Annual Exhibition* XXII-XXV (1909-12); vol. XXVIII (1915) contains a drawing from the Bennett-Rebori atelier.

27. E. L. Birch, "Advancing the Art and Science of Planning. Planners and Their Organizations. 1909-1980," *APAJ* XLVI (Jan. 1980), pp. 23-25; R. Van Nest Black, *Planning and the Planning Profession. The Past Fifty Years, 1917-1967* (Washington, 1967), pp. 6, 19-20; M. Scott, *American City Planning Since 1890* (Berkeley, 1971), pp. 163-66.

28. Scott (note 27), p. 141.

29. F. L. Olmsted, "President's Address of Welcome," *Proceedings of the Third National Conference on City Planning*, Philadelphia, May 15-17, 1911 (Boston, 1911), p. 12.

30. On planning in Bennett's day, see J. L. Hancock, "Planners in the Changing American City, 1900-1940," *AIPJ* XXXIII (Sept. 1967), pp. 290-304; P. Marcuse, "Housing Policy and City Planning: the Puzzling Split in the United States, 1893-1931," and B. A. Brownell, "Urban Planning, the Planning Profession, and the Motor Vehicle in Early Twentieth Century America," in *Shaping an Urban World*, ed. Gordon Cherry (New York, 1980), pp. 23-77.

31. EHB, "City Planning," in American Institute of Architects, Committee on Education, *The Significance of the Fine Arts* (Boston, [1923]), p. 361. See also EHB, "Public Buildings and Quasi-Public Buildings," in *City Planning*, ed. John Nolen (New York and London, 1929), pp. 103-16; and the following typescripts of addresses in the EHB Papers: "Courses in Citizenship" (Cornell University, March 1915), "Zoning Discussion" (American Civic Association Annual Meeting, Philadelphia, October 29, 1919), "Zoning" (Zone Plan Conference, Chicago, December 16-17, 1919), "City Planning" (Duluth, 1934).

32. See Akeley (note 22), p. 56; W. D. Moody, *What of the City? America's Greatest Issue—City Planning. What It Is and How to Go About It to Achieve Success* (Chicago, 1919), p. 359; Walker (note 22), p. 264; H. Whitehead, ed., *The Chicago Plan Commission, a Historical Sketch: 1909-1960* (Chicago, 1961).

33. Moody (note 32), p. 68.

34. EHB Diary, January 28-29, 1913; Chicago Plan Commission, *Proceedings of the Fifth Meeting of the Executive Committee . . . April 22, 1910*, p. 86.

35. Moody (note 32), p. 4.

36. See W. D. Moody, *Wacker's Manual of the Plan of Chicago: Political Economy* (Chicago, 1911); Chicago Plan Commission, *Chicago's Greatest Issue: An Official Plan* (Chicago, 1911); idem, *Inventory of Publications, Chicago Plan Commission and Department of City Planning from 1909 through 1962* (Chicago, 1962); idem, *Chicago's World-Wide Influence in City Planning* (Chicago, 1914); C. H. Wacker, "Gaining Support for a City Planning Movement," *Proceedings of the Fifth National Conference on City Planning*, Chicago, May 5-7, 1913 (Boston, 1913), p. 222-43. See also Akeley (note 22); T. J. Schlereth, "Moody's go-getting Wacker Manual," *Inland Architect* XXIV (April 1980), pp. 9-11.

37. "Address by Charles H. Wacker at a Meeting of the Chicago Plan Commission, November 4, 1926," excerpt from *Proceedings, Twenty-Eighth Meeting: November 4, 1926*.

38. All information on the Monroe Street Bridge has been garnered from EHB Diaries, June 9, 1912, March 14, and May 11-18, 1914; October 10, 1916; B. Holden (EHB employee) to EHB, October 23, 1911; EHB to E. B. Butler, May 13, 1914; WEP to E. B. Butler, May 29, 1914; letters in EHB Papers; EHB, "The Chicago River Bridges," *Arch. Rec.* LII (Dec. 1922), pp. 459-69; *The Economist* (Oct. 5, 1912), p. 582; *ibid.*, (Nov. 9, 1912), p. 787; *ibid.*, (Feb. 13, 1915), p. 280; *ibid.*, (Jan. 29, 1916), p. 227; *ibid.*, (Aug. 10, 1918), p. 243; "Work of the Municipal Art Committee, Illinois Chapter, A.I.A.," *ISAMB* II (March 1918), p. 3; "Report of the Municipal Art Committee, Illinois Chapter, A.I.A., June 11, 1918," *ISAMB* III (July 1918), p. 7; Chicago Plan Commission, *Proceedings of the Eighteenth Meeting of the Executive Committee . . . October 24, 1912*, p. 388; idem, *Proceedings of the Twenty-Sixth Meeting of the Executive Committee . . . March 10, 1914*, pp. 682-85; idem, *Sixth Annual Report and Proceedings of the Fourteenth Meeting . . . March 16, 1916*, p. 839; Chicago Department of Public Works, Bureau of Engineering, Division of Bridges and Viaducts, "Major Bridges Maintained (or Partly Maintained) by the Bureau of Engineering, Department of Public Works," typescript, 1968; D. N. Becker, "The Story of Chicago's Bridges," *Midwest Engineer* II (Jan. 1950), pp. 3-9.

39. Chicago Plan Commission, *Sixth Annual Report and Proceedings of the Fourteenth Meeting . . . March 16, 1916*, p. 832.

40. *Chicago Daily Tribune*, June 21, 1928, pp. 6-7.

41. Walker (note 22), pp. 246-49.

42. Chicago Plan Commission, *The Chicago Plan in 1933. Twenty-Five Years of Accomplishment* (Chicago, 1933); Chicago Department of Public Works, Bureau of Engineering, Division of Bridges and Viaducts, "List 1: Index of City Facilities Numbers," typescript, 1978.

43. EHB, "The Process of Working out a Zoning Program for Chicago" (address to American Civic Association, Chicago, Nov. 16, 1921), typescript, EHB Papers; HTF, "The Work of the Chicago Zoning Commission" (speech to Women's City Club, Chicago, April 24, 1922), typescript, EHB Papers; EHB, "Zoning Chicago," *National Municipal Review* XI (March 1922), pp. 69-71; C. B. Ball, "The Promotion of Zoning in Chicago," *American City* XXVI (Jan. 1923), pp. 11-14.

44. The South Park Commissioners approved the design of the fountain and paid for the basin. "Clarence Buckingham Memorial Fountain. Bennett Parsons and Frost Architects, Chicago," typescript, n.d., EHB Papers; EHB Diaries, January 26, November 6, 1923; January 29, May 14, 1924; January 19, 1925.

45. Chicago Plan Commission, *Proceedings of the Eighty-fourth Meeting of the Executive Committee . . . August 5, 1930*, p. 1425.

46. Chicago Plan Commission, *Proceedings of the Eightieth Meeting of the Executive Committee . . . March 21, 1930*, pp. 1394-96.

47. An east-west expressway was later built along the line of Congress Street. See Chicago Plan Commission, *Proceedings of the Eighty-second Meeting of the Executive Committee . . . May 29, 1930*, pp. 1416-17; EHB and HTF, *The Axis of Chicago. Congress Street Superhighway Compared with Other Projects* (Chicago, 1929), "Chicago Plan. The Streets Surrounding and Radiating from the Down Town District of Chicago. Principles involved in their Development. Downtown Quadrangles," mimeographed, June 12, 1929, EHB Papers; EHB to A.A. Sprague, July 22, 1928; HTF to EHB, December 6, 1928; EHB to West Side Street Improvement Committee, c.

December 1928; EHB to Chicago Plan Commission, October 3, 1929; D.F.W. Peck to EHB, December 5, 1929, EHB Papers. Newspaper coverage of the east-west axis question was extensive; see *Chicago Daily News,* December 27, 1926, April 16, May 21, 22, June 10, October 23, 1929; *Chicago Evening Post,* August 19, 1929, April 19, 1930; *Chicago Herald and Examiner,* September 19, October 5, 1929; *Chicago Tribune,* August 22, September 22, October 15, 16, 1929.

48. EHB Diary, January 22, 1931. The Post Office was dedicated in 1933. The long and complicated story of the Post Office site involves not only bureaucratic intransigence and some dubious real estate transactions, but also the location and construction of Union Station, completed in 1925. The 1914 Union Station Ordinance prohibited blocking Congress Street and required the railroads to pay for a 200 foot-wide viaduct across the tracks. Thus, the Post Office, which is built over Union Station Company air-rights, has a hole cut through it. Subsequently, Congress Street was again endorsed as the route of the west side highway by a 1935 Division of Highways report. When the Congress Expressway (later Eisenhower Expressway) was constructed in the early 1950s, the concourse through the Post Office merely needed some widening. See Chicago Plan Commission, *Discussion of the Proposed Site and Type of Building for the West Side Post Office in Chicago* (Chicago, 1915); "Importance of Chicago's Postal Problem in the Scheme of Commercial Expansion," *Fine Arts Journal* XXXVI (March 1916), pp. 99-111; "Near West Side Site Proposed for Civic Hall," *Chicago Tribune,* April 23, 1930; W. A. Dudley to EHB, June 30, 1930, including "Story of the Purchase of the New Postoffice Site," EHB Papers; Illinois Division of Highways (Charles DeLeuw), "Report on the Development of a Major Traffic Artery on the West Side of the City of Chicago," mimeographed, February 1935; "Superhighway Developments in the Chicago Area," *Midwest Engineer* II (Jan. 1950), pp. 10-12; *Chicago Tribune,* June 22, 1974.

49. The representative from Detroit was Charles Moore, editor of the Chicago Plan. See Detroit City Plan and Improvement Commission, *A Center of Arts and Letters. Report of Joint Committee . . . with plans prepared by Edward H. Bennett and Frank Miles Day* (Detroit, 1913); EHB, *Preliminary Plan of Detroit* (Detroit, 1915); "Detroit Plans its Future," *ASPO Newsletter* XIX (Oct. 1953), pp. 73-74; W. H. Ferry, *The Buildings of Detroit. A History* (Detroit, 1968), pp. 217, 220-21, 358, 368.

50. EHB, *The Greater Portland Plan* (Portland, 1912); EHB, untitled address in Portland, March 4, 1912, typescript, EHB Papers. See also H. K. Menhinick, "City Planning in Portland, Oregon," *City Planning* V (April 1929), p. 72; S. Dotterrer, "Cities and Towns," in *Space, Style and Structure. Building in Northwest America,* T. Vaughan and V. G. Ferriday, eds. (Portland, 1974), II, pp. 448-52; Portland Bureau of Planning, *The Portland Planning Commission, an Historical Overview* (Portland, 1979), pp. 8-11.

51. Minneapolis Civic Commission, *The Plan of Minneapolis . . . by Edward H. Bennett, architect; edited and written by Andrew Wright Crawford, Esq.* (Minneapolis, 1917); EHB, "Preliminary Report of the Minneapolis Civic Commission," *Western Architect* XVII (Jan. 1917), pp. 17-19; EHB, "The New Minneapolis Plan," *Architectural Review* XXIII (April 1918), p. 55-58.

52. Only Bernard Maybeck's Palace of Fine Arts remained. On the plan, see W. Polk, "The Ground Plan of the Exposition," *Commonwealth Club Transactions* [San Francisco] X (Aug. 1915), pp. 348-57; on the fate of the fairgrounds see M. M. O'Shaughnessey, "Exposition Grounds Replanned as a Restricted Residence Park," *American City* XVII (Jan. 1918), pp. 77-79; on the Palace of Fine Arts, see B. M. Maybeck, *Palace of Fine Arts and Lagoon, Panama-Pacific International Exposition, 1915* (San Francisco, 1915); on the fair, see L. C. Mullgardt, *The Architecture and Landscape Gardening of the Exposition* (San Francisco, 1915), and F. M. Todd, *The Story of the Exposition,* 5 vols. (New York and London, 1921).

53. *Elgin Gazette,* December 7, 1910, and April 4, 12, 1911; Cedar Rapids City Plan Commission, *Comprehensive City Plan for Cedar Rapids, Iowa* (Cedar Rapids, 1931), pp. 9, 122-96; EHB, *Plan of Elgin* (Chicago, 1917), p. 34. Drawings prepared for the Riverfront Improvement Commission are in the Department of Planning and Redevelopment, Cedar Rapids.

54. EHB, "Report on the General Plan for the Borough of Brooklyn," typescript, 1914, EHB Papers; "The Story of Brooklyn's City Plan," *The Brooklyn Daily Eagle,* January 18, 1914.

55. Federal Plan Commission, *Report of the Federal Plan Commission on A General Plan for the Cities of Ottawa and Hull* (Ottawa, 1915); EHB, "A Plan for Ottawa, the Capital of the Dominion of Canada," *AIAJ* IV (June 1916), pp. 263-65. See also National Capital Planning Service, Jacques Greber, Consultant, *Plan for the National Capital. General Report* (Ottawa, 1950), pp. 133-38; W. Van Nus, "The Fate of City Beautiful Thought in Canada, 1893-1930," in *The Canadian City: Essays in Urban History,* G. A. Stelter and A. F. J. Artibise, eds. (Toronto, 1977), pp. 162-85; W. Eggleston, *The Queen's Choice: A Story of Canada's Capitol* (Ottawa, 1961), 154-70.

56. R. C. Alberts, *The Shaping of the Point. Pittsburgh's Renaissance Park* (Pittsburgh, 1980), pp. 9-40, 79, 193, 202.

57. E. Arpee, *Lake Forest, Illinois, History and Reminiscences, 1861-1961* (Lake Forest, 1964), p. 144.

58. For Cyrus McCormick he made a plan for McCormick Seminary (1911-12); Harold McCormick discussed with Bennett a plan for Lake Forest (1909); Mrs. McKinlock commissioned a plan for Palm Beach (1929-30); Charles Dewey was assistant Secretary of the Treasury when Bennett was appointed architect for new government buildings in Washington (1926-27).

59. David Benton Jones (1848-1923) was a Princeton-trained lawyer, later President of the Mineral Point Zinc Company. His house and its barn still exist. See *Chicago Tribune,* August 24, 1923; Arpee (note 57), p. 146; "A Bright New World in a Greek Revival Dairy Barn," *House Beautiful* CX (May 1968), pp. 116-21.

60. Correspondence, specifications, and photographs, EHB Papers; working drawings in the possession of EHB, Jr.

61. Arpee (note 57), pp. 179-80; EHB Diary, October 25, 1912.

62. W. S. Dobyns, *California Gardens* (New York, 1931), pls. 33, 109; R. Pratt, *David Adler* (New York, 1970), pp. 58-59; D. Gebhard to author, July 20, 1980.

63. EHB, "Report of E. H. Bennett, Consulting Architect on the General Plan of Camp Grant, Rockford, Ill. . . ," typescript, December 1917, and "Completion Report, Camp Knox, Kentucky . . .," typescript, September 1, 1919, EHB Papers; E. Rische, *Quartermaster Support of the Army: History of the Corps 1775-1939* (Washington, D.C., 1962); Scott (note 27), p. 170.

64. Bennett was indirectly connected with the civic centers in both Cleveland and San Francisco through the Burnham plan for the former city (1902-03) and through his long advocacy of his and Burnham's scheme for the latter, which was not the one selected when construction began in 1912.

65. C. M. Robinson, "Opening the Center of Denver," *Arch. Rec.* XIX (May 1906), pp. 365-67; idem, "The Development of Denver," *American City* II (1910), pp. 196-201; "History of Denver's Projected Civic Center," *Denver Municipal Facts* I (October 2, 1909), pp. 3-7, 10-12; F. L. Olmsted, "Plans of Developing Civic Center Outlined by Landscape Architect," *Denver Municipal Facts* I (April 1913), pp. 3-6; T. M. Fisher, "The Denver Civic Center" *Arch. Rec.* LIII (March 1923), pp. 189-201; *Rocky Mountain News,* March 23, 1913, April 2, 1918, December 11, 1921; V. McConnell, "For These High Purposes," *Colorado Magazine* XLIV (Summer 1969), pp. 204-23; J. P. Mitchell, "Boss Speer and the City Functional. Boosters and Businessmen versus Commission Government in Denver," *Pacific Northwest Quarterly* CXIII (October 1972), pp. 155-64.

66. These statistics are taken from T. K. Hubbard, "Survey of City and Regional Planning in the United States, 1924," *City Planning* I (April 1925), p. 7; T. K. Hubbard and H. V. Hubbard, *Our Cities To-day and To-morrow* (Cambridge, Mass., 1929), p. 3; Scott (note 27), p. 229.

67. Brownell (note 30); Scott (note 27), pp. 110-269.

68. The Minneapolis plan was privately printed, a fact that in part accounts for its lavish design. Also, earlier schemes for an axial boulevard leading to Cass Gilbert's 1905 State Capitol made further elaborations of this sort unnecessary. See EHG, WEP, and G. H. Herrold, *Plan of Saint Paul* (St. Paul, 1922); Herrold to EHB, June 20, 1929, and John Druar to EHB, June 21, 1929, EHB Papers; G. H. Herrold, "St. Pauls's Changing Riverfront," *City Planning* VI (Oct. 1930), pp. 283-88; G. Bundlie, "St. Paul Moves Forward," *City Planning* XII (Oct. 1931), pp. 313-24; G. H. Herrold, "Replanning Moves Forward in St. Paul," *American City* LIII (March 1938), pp. 41-42.

69. EHB, *Plan of Winnetka* (n.p., 1921), and "The Proposed City Plan of Winnetka, Illinois," *American City* XXI (Oct. 1919), pp. 305-07.

70. Bennett, Parsons and Frost, "Tentative Report . . . Proposing Zoning Ordinance for the City of Lake Forest," typescript, June 11, 1923; EHB, "Lake Forest, Illinois. Preliminary Report on the City Plan," typescript, 1929; "Lake Forest, the Major Highway along the Main Line of the C. & N.W. Railway to Relieve Sheridan Road," typescript, n.d.; HTF, "The North Shore . . . A Study of Traffic Conditions . . . Recommendations," typescript, October 20, 1938; "An Analysis of Traffic Routes for the Northshore . . . ," typescript, n.d.; EHB, "Northshore Property Owners. An Ideal for the North Shore," typescript, n.d., but printed in *Chicago Tribune,* December 12, 1937; "The North Shore," typescript, n.d.; correspondence between EHB and Lake Forest Plan Commission, 1926-39, EHB Papers.

71. D. H. Burnham, Jr., and R. Kingery, *Planning the Region of Chicago* (Chicago, 1956), pp. 84-95.

72. Committee on the Regional Plan of New York and Its Environs, *Regional Survey of New York and Its Environs,* 8 vols. (New York, 1927-31); idem, *Regional Plan of New York and Its Environs,* vol. 1, *The Graphic Regional Plan*; vol. 2, T. Adams, assisted by H. M. Lewis and L. M. Orton, *The Building of the City* (New York, 1929-31).

73. Committee on the Regional Plan of New York and Its Environs, *The Plan of New York with References to the Chicago Plan, Letter from Charles D. Norton to Frederic A. Delano* (New York, 1923), quoted in D. A. Johnson, "The Emergence of Metropolitan Regionalism: An Analysis of the 1929 Regional Plan of New York and Its Environs" (Ph.D. diss., Cornell, 1974), p. 118.

74. EHB, "Plan of New York and Its Environs, Sector 6," typescript, June 15, 1923; two maps of Sector 6; "Plan of New York and Its Environs—Reports on Preliminary Survey of Six Sectors Comprising the Environs of New York and Having an Area of 4900 Square Miles," typescript, October 1923, EHB Papers. See also H. A. Kantor, "Charles Dyer Norton and the Origins of the Regional Plan of New York," *AIPJ* XXXIX (Jan. 1973), p. 40; Johnson (note 73), pp. 176-220.

75. Johnson (note 73), pp. 214-15.

76. L. Mumford, "The Plan of New York," *New Republic* LXXI (June 15, 1932), pp. 121-26, and "The Plan of New York, II," *New Republic* LXXI (June 22, 1932), pp. 146-53; Kantor (note 74), p. 41; Johnson (note 73), pp. 3-5, 9, 376-81.

77. Papers, photographs, and drawings pertaining to all these commissions can be found in the EHB Papers and Diaries.

78. M. Barnes, "Tiffin, Ohio, 1885-1976," typescript, 1976, Tiffin-Seneca Public Library, Tiffin, Ohio, pp. 9-11.

79. EHB, "Pasadena, The Grouping of Civic Buildings," typescript, 1923; Bennett, Parsons and Frost, "Report on a Plan for the City of Pasadena, California," typescript, April 30, 1925, EHB Papers; F. Thomas, "How the Civic Plan of Pasadena was Evolved," *California Southland* VI (Nov. 1924), pp. 9-10; H. Wadsworth, "The City Plans of Pasadena," *California Southland* V (May 1923), pp. 7-8; Pasadena Heritage, "Pasadena Civic Center District," a National Register of Historic Places Nomination, typescript, September 15, 1978, Community Development Department, City of Pasadena.

80. WEP, "The George Rogers Clark Memorial," *American City* L (April 1935), pp. 47-48; U.S. Department of the Interior, National Park Service, Office of History and Historic Architecture, *George Rogers Clark Na-*

tional Historical Park, Vincennes, Indiana, George Rogers Clark Memorial. Historic Structures Report. Historical Data, by E. C. Bearss (Washington, D.C., 1970).

81. A plan of the New Orleans City Park is in the Art Institute of Chicago's collection (Department of Architecture). See also *Morning Tribune* (New Orleans), December 14, 1931; American Institute of Architects, New Orleans Chapter, *A Guide to New Orleans Architecture* (New Orleans, 1974), p. 113; M. L. Christovich, S. K. Evans, and R. Toledano, *New Orleans Architecture,* V, *The Esplanade Ridge* (Gretna, La., 1977), p. 140.

82. L. Skidmore, "Planning and Planners," *Architectural Forum* LIX (July 1933), pp. 29-32; L. R. Lohr, *Fair Management, The Story of A Century of Progress Exposition: A Guide for Future Fairs* (Chicago, 1952), pp. 60-61; C. Condit, *Chicago 1930-70. Building, Planning, and Urban Technology* (Chicago and London, 1974), pp. 3-6.

83. "Preliminary Studies for the Chicago World's Fair," *Pencil Points* X (April 1929), pp. 217-28; Lohr (note 82), pp. 61-64.

84. EHB Diary, May 3, July 2, 1929; " 'A Century of Progress,' Members of Architectural Committee for Chicago's Centennial Celebration Submit Second Set of Sketches," *Western Architect* XXXVIII (June 1929), pp. 91-98; Lohr (note 82), p. 64.

85. Lohr (note 82), pp. 65-71, 130-31, 146-52, 226-33; A Century of Progress, Inc., *Official Guide Book of the Fair* (Chicago, 1933), pp. 195, 208-13, 221-23; Condit (note 82), pp. 8-17.

86. EHB Diaries, April 24, 1925; September 20, October 22, 1926; May 23, July 13, 1927; J. A. Wetmore to C. S. Dewey, March 28, 1927; C. Moore to A. W. Mellon, April 5, 1927; and C. S. Dewey to A. W. Mellon, May 12, 1927, General Correspondence, Board of Architectural Consultants, Public Buildings Service, Record Group 121, National Archives, Washington, D.C.; A. N. Marquis, *Book of Chicagoans* (Chicago, 1917), p. 185; F. Gutheim, *Worthy of the Nation. The History of Planning for the National Capital* (Washington, D.C., 1977), pp. 159-75.

87. The quotations about style are from EHB Diary, April 13, 1931; Mellon's suggestions on planning are quoted in EHB, "The Architecture of the Capital," in *The Development of the United States Capital,* 71st Cong., 1st sess. H. Doc. No. 35, 1930. See also EHB Diaries, February 4, 1929, May 27, 1932; EHB, "The New Departmental Buildings in Washington, D.C.," typescript, n.d., and "The Great Plaza Chronological Record," typescript, December 7, 1933, EHB Papers; H. W. Peaslee to C. S. Dewey, December 3, 1927; L. A. Simon to EHB, February 13, 1928; L. A. Simon to W. A. Delano, November 7, 1928; L. A. Simon to EHB, November 27, 1929; C. Moore to EHB, November 20, 1929; L. A. Simon to A. W. Mellon, November 30, 1929, General Correspondence, Board of Architectural Consultants; Commission of Fine Arts, *Minutes,* November 18, 1929-December 15, 1933; Gutheim (note 86), pp. 175-79.

88. EHB, "The New Departmental Buildings in Washington, D.C." (note 87), p. 7.

89. See memorandum to Director of Procurement, June 14, 1935, General Correspondence, Board of Architectural Consultants; Gutheim (note 86), pp. 180, 182. H. Weese and Associates, *The Master Plan for the Federal Triangle: Historic Report* (Washington, 1981), pp. 23-24.

90. EHB Diaries, February 14, 1934; January 29, 1935; April 11, 1935; April 29, 1935; L. W. Roberts to W. A. Delano, January 27, 1934, General Correspondence, Board of Architectural Consultants; "Cabinet Sketches," Apex Buildings Drawings, Cartographic Department, National Archives; The Dunlop Society, B. Lowry, ed., "The Federal Triangle," in *The Architecture of Washington, D.C.,* vol. II (microfiche) (Washington, D.C., 1979).

91. On the exhibitions of Bennett's paintings, see, for example, *Chicago Tribune,* November 22, 1940; March 2, 1941; *Chicago Daily News,* November 25, 1946; June 14, 1948. Bennett's obituaries are to be found in the *Chicago Tribune,* October 16, 1954; *The Lake Forester,* October 21, 1954. Bennett died October 14, 1954, in Tryon, N.C.

92. The entire quotation is to be found in Moore (note 10), II, p. 147. Burnham's famous dictum, however, was apparently assembled by his associate Willis Polk from various talks and letters.

Catalogue

1.
Marcel Loyau (1895-1936), *Edward H. Bennett,* 1927. Bronze portrait bust mounted on marble base, 57 x 31 x 23 cm. Lent by Mr. and Mrs. Edward H. Bennett, Jr.

2.
Edward H. Bennett's Certificate of Architectural Registration in the State of Illinois, dated December 6, 1912, and signed by N. Clifford Ricker, President, and Peter B. Wight, Secretary and Treasurer, of the Illinois Society of Architects. Lithograph and collage, 53 x 38.6 cm. Gift of Edward H. Bennett, Jr., 1973.

3.
Edward H. Bennett, *Elevation of the Royal Portal of the West Facade, Chartres Cathedral,* 1896. Pencil and watercolor on paper, approx. 95 x 61 cm. Lent by Mr. and Mrs. Edward H. Bennett, Jr.

4.
Edward H. Bennett, *Elevation of the Northwest Bay of the North Portal, Chartres Cathedral,* 1896. Pencil and watercolor on paper, approx. 82.5 x 57 cm. Lent by Mr. and Mrs. Edward H. Bennett, Jr.

5.
Edward H. Bennett, *Travel Sketches of St. Mary Dalton and St. Martin-in-the-Fields, London,* c. 1897-99. Pencil on paper, each 20.5 x 12.7 cm. Gifts of Edward H. Bennett, Jr., 1973.

6.
Menu for the Patron's Dinner at Atelier Bennett, Chicago, 18 June 1908. Blueprint, 46.5 x 16 cm. Gift of Edward H. Bennett, Jr., 1973.

7.
Chicago. Plan of the Complete System of Street Circulation. Published as plate 110 in Daniel H. Burnham and Edward H. Bennett, *The Plan of Chicago* (Chicago: R. R. Donnelley for the Commercial Club, 1909). Ink and wash on paper, 103 x 100 cm. On permanent loan from the City of Chicago, Department of Development and Planning.

8.
Chicago. Plan of a Complete System of Street Circulation and Systems of Parks and Playgrounds ... Published as plate 85 in Daniel H. Burnham and Edward H. Bennett, *The Plan of Chicago* (Chicago: R. R. Donnelley for the Commercial Club, 1909), with annotations by Edward H. Bennett to show street and recreation projects executed by 1925. Colored pencil on colored halftone print, 28 x 35.5 cm. Gift of Edward H. Bennett, Jr., 1973.

3

5

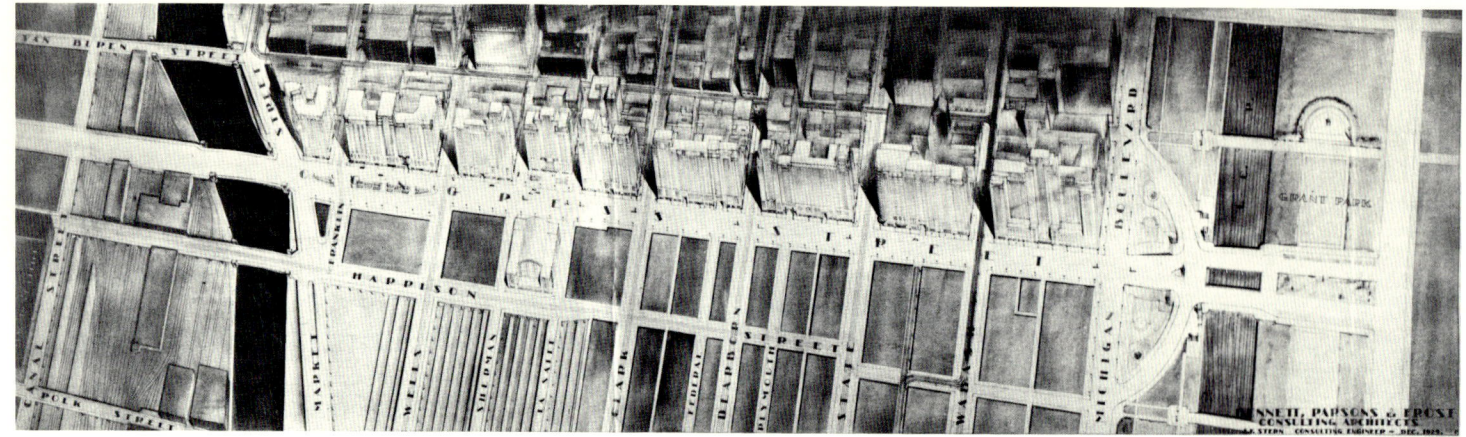

9

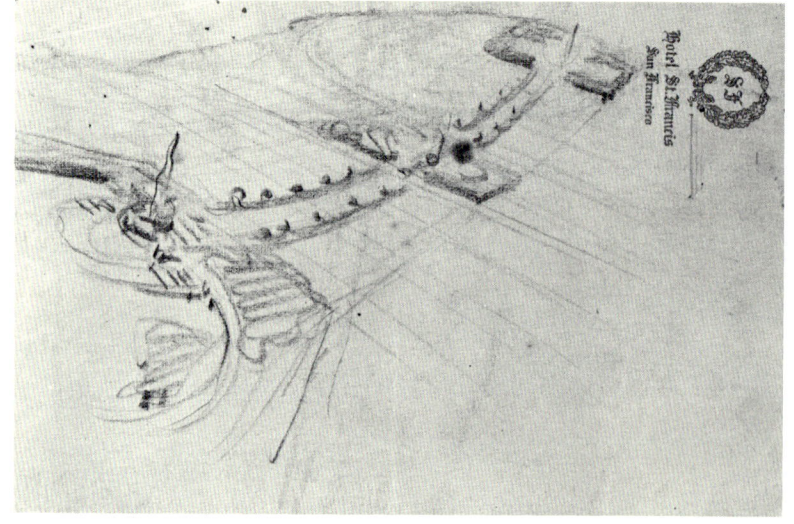

12

9.
Chicago. Congress Street. Bird's-Eye View of the Proposed Development between the Lake and the River. Bennett, Parsons and Frost, Consulting Architects, and I. F. Stern, Consulting Engineer, December 1929. Photostat, 21.3 x 64.7 cm. Gift of Edward H. Bennett, Jr., 1973.

10.
Edward H. Bennett, *Sketch for Chatham Fields, 81st Street and Cottage Grove Avenue, Chicago,* c. 1914-15. Colored pencil on tracing paper, 30 x 40 cm. Gift of Edward H. Bennett, Jr., 1973.

11.
Jules Guérin (1866-1946), *Minneapolis. The Sixth Avenue Artery,* c. 1910. Frontispiece from Edward H. Bennett and Andrew Wright Crawford, *The Plan of Minneapolis* (Minneapolis Civic Commission, 1917). Colored halftone print, 31.5 x 24 cm. Gift of Edward H. Bennett, Jr., 1973.

14

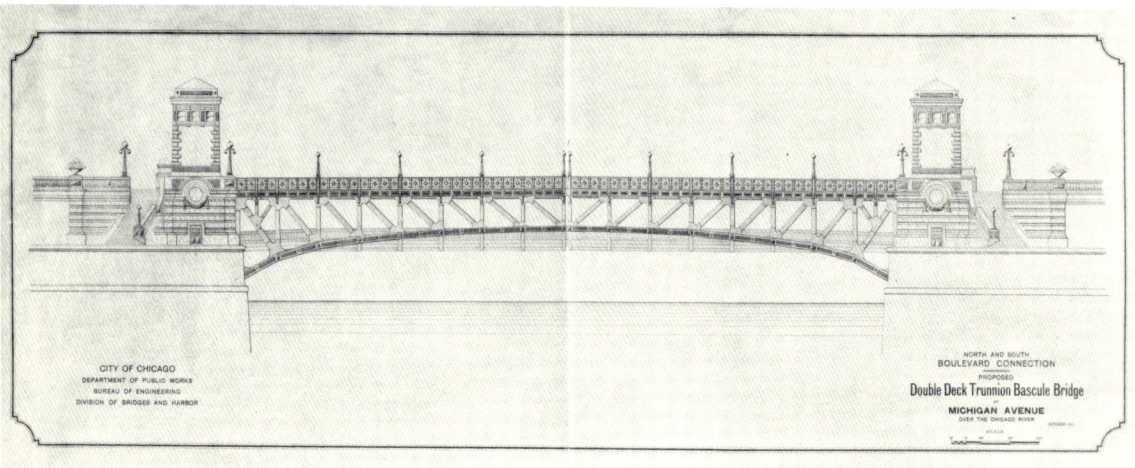

50

12.
Edward H. Bennett, *Sketch of a Boulevard, probably Market Street, from Twin Peaks, for San Francisco*, c. 1904. Pencil on note paper, 13.7 x 21.2 cm. Gift of Edward H. Bennett, Jr., 1973.

13.
Chicago. View looking North on the South Branch of the Chicago River Showing the Suggested Arrangements of Streets..., annotated "D. H. Burnham & E. H. Bennett—Consultants—1908." Published as plate 107 in Daniel H. Burnham and Edward H. Bennett, *The Plan of Chicago* (Chicago: R. R. Donnelley for the Commercial Club, 1909). Ink on colored halftone print mounted on paper and linen, 27.7 x 35.5 cm. Gift of Edward H. Bennett, Jr., 1973.

14.
Proposed Double Deck Trunnion Bascule Bridge at Michigan Avenue over the Chicago River, October 1912. Ink on linen, 59 x 131.5 cm. Lent by the City of Chicago, Department of Public Works.

15.
"The Big Stick and the Hand that Wields It," cartoon by F. H. Brottz, from *North-West Side Commercial Association Monthly Bulletin* IV, no. 11 (Nov. 1914), p. 1. Photolithograph, 29.7 x 22.2 cm. Gift of Edward H. Bennett, Jr., 1973.

16.
Jules Guérin, *Minneapolis. The Riverfront or "The Greatest of All Opportunities of Minneapolis."* Plate between pp. 150-51 from Edward H. Bennett and Andrew Wright Crawford, *The Plan of Minneapolis* (1917). Colored halftone print, 31.5 x 47 cm. Gift of Edward H. Bennett, Jr., 1973.

17.
Edward H. Bennett, *Perspective Sketch of the Proposed Shore Development Adjusted to Existing Bridges, Cedar Rapids, Iowa*, c. 1916. Ink on paper, 74.5 x 112 cm. Lent by the City of Cedar Rapids.

18.
Edward H. Bennett, *Tentative Plan for the River Front Improvement Commission, Cedar Rapids, Iowa*, July 3, 1916. Pencil and colored pencil on tracing paper, 82.5 x 106.8 cm. Lent by the City of Cedar Rapids.

15

17

19.
Chicago. Bird's-Eye View of Congress Street Extension and Post Office Site. Future Public Buildings as Suggested, Offices of Bennett, Parsons and Frost, December 20, 1926. Photostat, 64.3 x 46 cm. Gift of Edward H. Bennett, Jr., 1953.

20.
Edward H. Bennett, *Sketch Elevation of a Proposed Chicago Post Office from Congress Street*, c. 1930. Pencil on tracing paper, 24 x 38 cm. Gift of Edward H. Bennett, Jr., 1973.

21.
Elevation of a Proposed Chicago Terminal Station for the Lewis Plan, designed by Bennett and Frost, 1939. Pencil on tracing paper, 48 x 54 cm. Gift of Edward H. Bennett, Jr., 1953.

22.
Plan of a Proposed Chicago Terminal Station for the Lewis Plan, designed by Bennett and Frost, 1939. Pencil and colored pencil on tracing paper, 61 x 45.7 cm. Gift of Edward H. Bennett, Jr., 1953.

23.
Marcel Vilain (1879-?), *Minneapolis. The Civic Plaza and Civic Design*, designed by Edward H. Bennett, c. 1910-11. Plate p. 57 from Edward H. Bennett and Andrew Wright Crawford, *The Plan of Minneapolis* (1917). Halftone print, 31.5 x 24 cm. Gift of Edward H. Bennett, Jr., 1973.

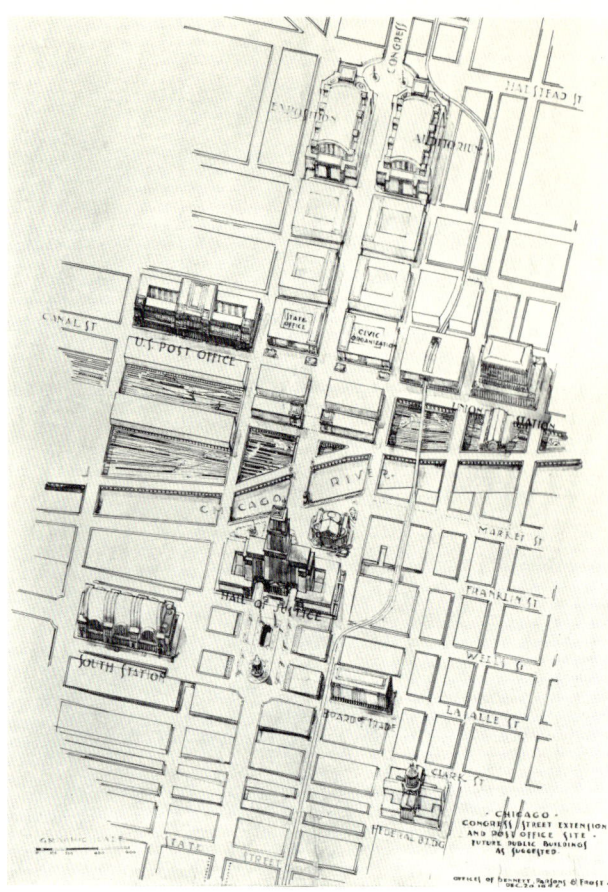

19

20

21

23

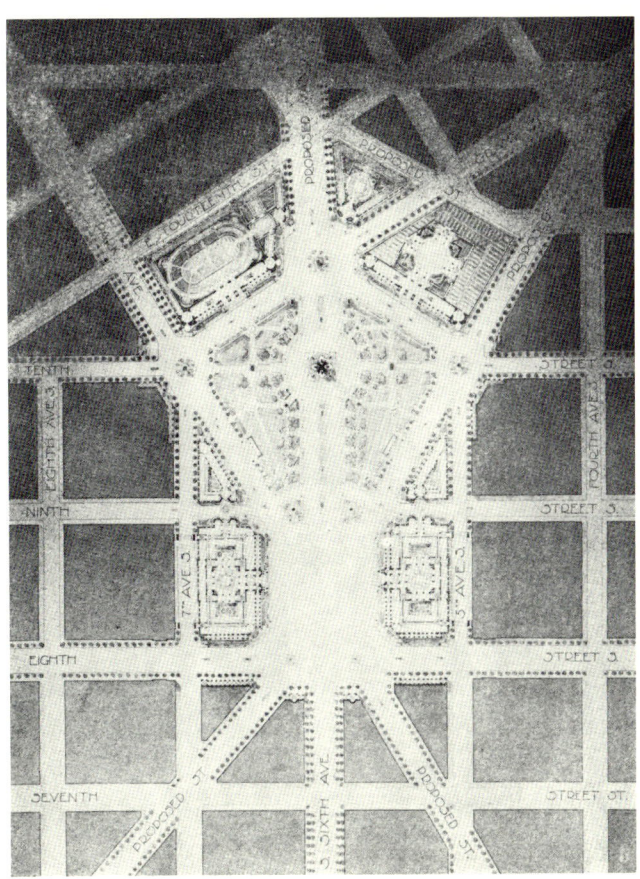

24.
Jules Guérin, *Bird's-Eye View of the Denver Civic Center*, designed by Bennett and Parsons, 1917. Colored halftone print, 21.6 x 28 cm. Gift of Edward H. Bennett, Jr., 1973.

25.
Bennett, Parsons, Frost and Thomas, *Pasadena Civic Center, Alternative Plan of Herkimer Street Extension*, May 1923. Ink and pencil on paper, 38.3 x 52.2 cm. Lent by the City of Pasadena.

26.
Washington, D.C. Perspective Rendering of the Apex Commissions Building, designed by Bennett, Parsons and Frost, 1931, from *Cabinet Sketches Comprising Plans, Elevations, Sections, and Perspective View of the Proposed Apex Commissions Building in the Triangle*, limited edition presentation portfolio, 1931. Etching, 58 x 91 cm. Gift of Edward H. Bennett, Jr., 1953.

27.
Chicago. General Plan of Grant Park, designed by Edward H. Bennett and drawn and traced by J.F.B., December 1925. Ink on linen, 51 x 99 cm. Gift of the City of Chicago, Chicago Park District.

28.
Plan, Section, Elevation, and Details of Buckingham Memorial Fountain, Chicago, designed by Bennett, Parsons and Frost, and J. H. Lambert, Associate Architect, May 6, 1925. Ink on linen, 67 x 95 cm. Gift of Edward H. Bennett, Jr., 1953.

29.
Marcel Loyau, *Two Maquettes for the Sea Horses, Buckingham Fountain*, 1927. Bronze mounted on limestone base, each 25.5 x 56 x 13 cm. Lent by Mr. and Mrs. Edward H. Bennett, Jr.

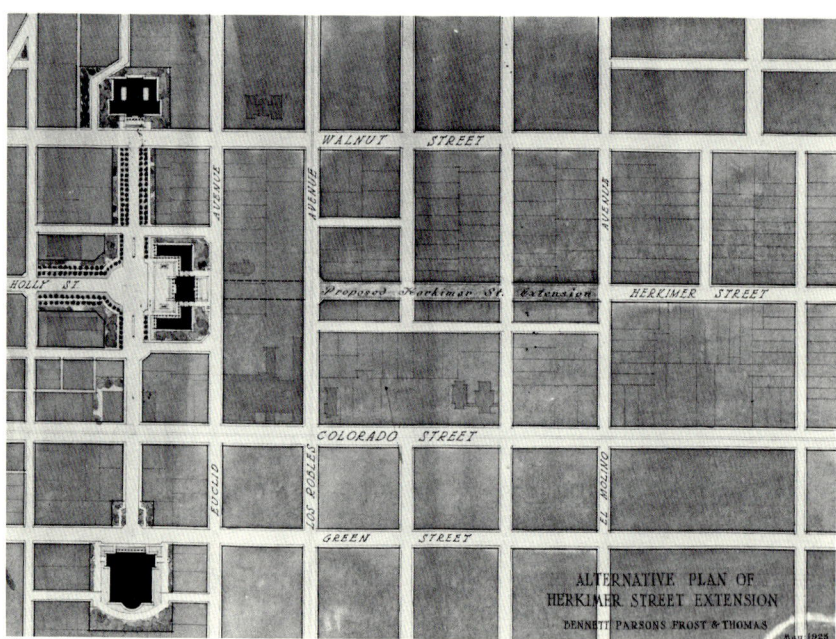

26

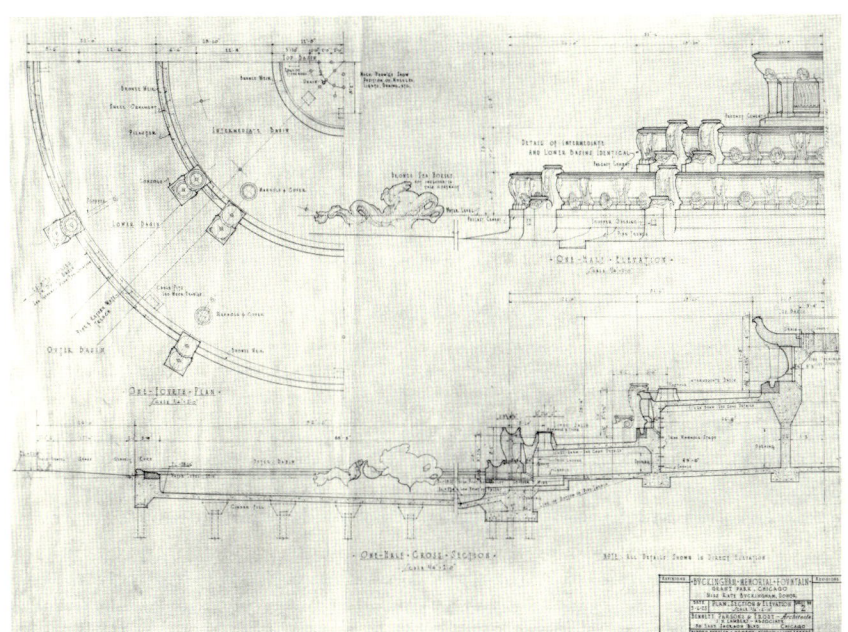

28

29

30

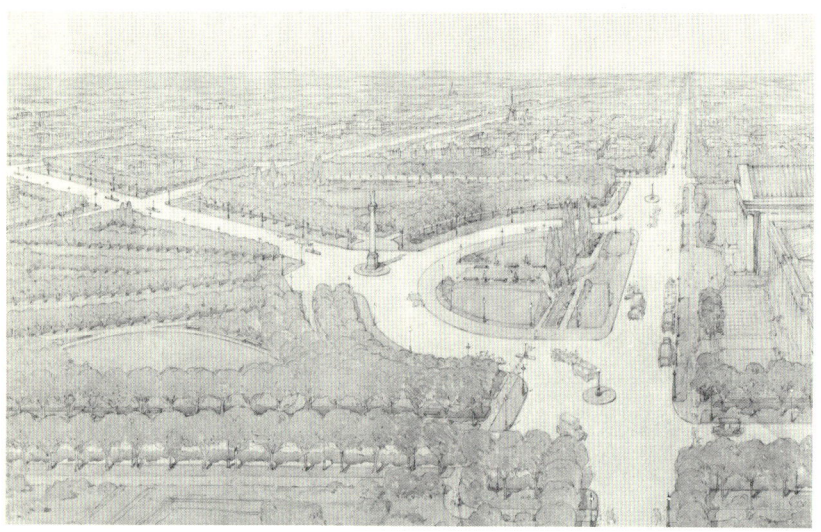

31

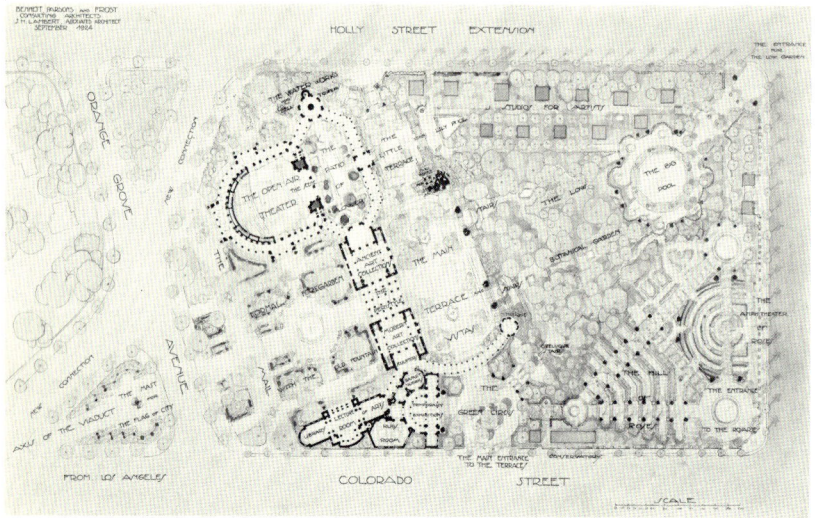

33

30.
Attributed to Marcel Vilain, *Minneapolis. Perspective of the Park in Front of the Art Museum at 24th Street Showing the Diagonal Approach from the Civic Center*, c. 1911. Watercolor on paper, approx. 50 x 77 cm. Lent by the City of Minneapolis, Records Management Division.

31.
Bennett, Parsons and Frost, Consulting Architects, J. H. Lambert, Associated Architect, *Plan of Carmelita Park, Pasadena*, September 1924. Ink and watercolor on paper mounted on illustration board, 41 x 66.5 cm. Lent by the City of Pasadena.

32.
Cover from the booklet of *Official Pictures of a Century of Progress Exposition* (Chicago: R. H. Donnelley Corp., 1933), showing the Travel and Transport Building designed by Edward H. Bennett, John Holabird, and Hubert Burnham. Colored halftone print, 25.5 x 18 cm. Anonymous gift, 1980.

33.
Weimer Pursell, Poster for the Century of Progress Exposition in Chicago, 1933, showing the Federal Building designed by Edward H. Bennett. Lithograph printed by Neely Printing Co., 104.1 x 68.5 cm. Lent by the Kelmscott Gallery, Chicago.

34.
Edward H. Bennett, *Plan and Bird's-Eye View Sketches*, c. 1911, of the Panama-Pacific International Exposition, San Francisco, 1915. Pencil and ink on note paper, 13.5 x 22.7 and 15.2 x 21.2 cm. Gifts of Edward H. Bennett, Jr., 1973.

35.
Bird's-Eye View of the Panama-Pacific International Exposition from Presidio Heights, San Francisco, 1915. Colored photolithograph printed by Cardinell-Vincent, 14.2 x 35.7 cm. Anonymous loan.

34

Appendix: List of Bennett's Work

Alphabetical listing of the work of Edward H. Bennett and his associates, giving inclusive dates. Dates in parentheses refer to publication of plans. An asterisk (*) has been used to indicate those commissions for which there are materials in the Bennett Papers or in other collections of the Art Institute of Chicago.

Bennett firms:

Edward H. Bennett, 1910-19

Edward H. Bennett and William E. Parsons, 1919-22

Bennett, Parsons, Frost & Thomas, 1922-24

Bennett, Parsons & Frost, 1924-38

Bennett & Frost, 1938-44

Arlington, Va.:
L'Enfant Memorial competition, March 1909, project*

Barnegat, N.J.:
Town site plan, January 1927, project*

Beloit, Wis.:
Beloit College plan, 1917, project

Bloomington, Ill.:
Civic Center, 1919, project*

Brooklyn, N.Y.:
City Plan, January 1912-April 1914, project*
Civic Center, 1915, project*

Buffalo, N.Y.:
City Plan and Public Building Sites (Civic Center), 1920-22, project*

Byron, Ill.:
Village Plan, 1919

Camp Grant, Ill.:
Cantonment, near Rockford, 1917*

Camp Knox, Ky.:
Cantonment, near Louisville, 1918-19*

Camp Las Casas, P.R.:
Cantonment, near San Juan, 1918

Cedar Rapids, Iowa:
River front plan, July 1910-April 1911, 1916

Chicago, Ill.:
Miscellaneous buildings and monuments:
    Alexander Hamilton Memorial 1927-29, project (with J. H. Lambert and M. Loyau)*
    The Art Institute of Chicago, addition, competition, 1934 project*
    Buckingham Fountain Grant Park, 1924-27 (with J. H. Lambert and M. Loyau)*
    Grant Park Stadium (Soldier Field), competition, 1919, project
    Marshall Field & Company, mosaic "dome," 1906 (with DHB)

Pasteur Memorial, now opposite Cook County Hospital, 1924-28
    (with L. Hermant, sculptor)*
St. Chrysostom's Church, consulting architects for remodeling, 1923-26
War Memorial in Grant Park, November 1918-January 1919, project*
Site plans and building groups:
    Century of Progress International Exposition, 1929-33*
        Site plan (with others)
        Administration Building (with Burnham and Holabird)
        Agricultural Building (with Brown)
        Dairy Building (with Brown)
        Federal Building
        Hall of States (with Brown)
        Travel and Transport Building (with Burnham and Holabird)
    Chatham Fields, South Park, and Englefield, South Side subdivisions, 1914-16*
    McCormick Seminary plan, April 1911-November 1912, project
For South Park District:
    Armour Square Fieldhouse 1904-05 (with DHB)
    Bessemer Park Fieldhouse, 1904-05 (with DHB)
    Burnham Park, preliminary plans, 1915-19
    Cornell Square Fieldhouse, 1904-05 (with DHB)
    Davis Square Fieldhouse, 1904-05, 1910 (with DHB)*
    Fuller Park Fieldhouse, 1904-11 (with DHB)*
    Grant Park, 1915-27*
    Hamilton Park Fieldhouse, reading room addition, 1904-10 (with DHB)*
    Ogden Park Fieldhouse, 1903-05 (with DHB)
    Palmer Park Fieldhouse, 1904-05 (with DHB)
    Russell Square Fieldhouse, 1903-05 (with DHB)
    Sherman Park Fieldhouse, 1903-05 (with DHB)
    Mark White Square (now McGuane Park) Fieldhouse, library extension,
        1904-10 (with DHB)*
    Washington Park, South Park District Administration Building (now DuSable
        Museum), 1908-10 (with DHB)*
    Street lamp standards for Michigan Avenue and elsewhere (with DHB and alone)*
For Chicago Plan Commission:
    The Chicago Plan, 1906-09 (1909) (with DHB)*
    Bridges (giving completion dates), consulting architect:
        Adams Street, August 26, 1927
        Belmont Avenue, July 12, 1917
        N. Central Park Avenue, 1913
        Clark Street, July 10, 1929
        S. Damen Avenue, October 4, 1930
        Franklin-Orleans, October 23, 1920
        N. Kedzie Avenue, 1914
        Lake Street, November 6, 1916
        LaSalle Street, December 20, 1928
        Madison Street, November 29, 1922
        Michigan Avenue, May 14, 1920*
        Monroe Street, February 22, 1919
        100th Street, 1927
        106th Street, 1929
        N. Ogden Avenue (2 bridges), December 9, 1932
        Roosevelt Road, September 13, 1928
        Wabash Avenue, December 30, 1930
        Washington Street, May 26, 1913

Wells Street, February 11, 1922
Wilson Avenue, 1914
Street widenings and extensions, consulting architect:
    Ashland Avenue widening, 1919 +
    Avondale Highway, 1927 +
    Canal Street widening for Union Station, 1913 +
    Congress Avenue, superhighway, 1927-29, project*
    Robey Avenue (now Damen Avenue) widening, 1910 +
    LaSalle Street widening, 1922 +
    N. Michigan Avenue widening and extension;
        plans, 1910 + ; widening construction, 1916 + ; extension construction, 1918 + *
    Ogden Avenue extension, 1916 +
    Outer Drive, preliminary design, 1927 +
    Roosevelt Road, plan, 1913; widening construction, 1916 +
    South Water and Market Streets (now Wacker Drive) plan, 1917; construction, 1924-26*
    Western Avenue widening, 1919 +
Building locations:
    Criminal Court Building site, 1924-25
    Field Museum site, 1911-14
    Post Office site negotiations, 1910-19
    Union Station negotiations, 1913
Zoning Ordinance and survey maps, 1923

Davenport, Iowa:
Zoning Ordinance, June 1925*

Denver, Col.:
Civic Center, February 1917*

Detroit, Mich.:
Center for Arts and Letters, (1913) (with F. M. Day)
City Plan, 1911-15 (1915)

Duluth, Minn.:
Memorial Hall Group Plan, 1923, project
Civic Center Plan, 1909 (with DHB)

Elgin, Ill.:
City Plan, March 1916-January 1917 (1917)*

Elkhart, Ind.:
St. Joseph Manor subdivision plan, September 1915*

Evanston, Ill.:
Northwestern University Development Plan, November 1927*

Flossmor, Ill.:
Flossmor Park subdivision plan, 1923, project (?)*

Fort Wayne, Ind.:
Zoning Ordinance, 1927-28*

Gary, Ind.:
City Plan, 1920-23*

Highland Park, Ill.:
City Plan, 1919-20

Joliet, Ill.:
City Plan, April 1919-21 (1921)*
Zoning Ordinance, 1927

Lake Forest, Ill.:
Zoning Ordinance, 1923*
City Plan, 1929*
"Bagatelle," E. H. Bennett house and garden, 1915-16*
Knollwood Country Club, site plan, 1924*

Miami, Fla.:
Biscayne Boulevard, lamp standards, competition advisor, 1926*

Milwaukee, Wis.:
Civic Center, 1922, project*

Minneapolis, Minn.:
City Plan, 1910-17 (1917)*

Montecito, Cal.:
"Pepper Hill," David B. Jones garden, 1915-16

New Orleans, La.:
City Park, 1933*

New York, N.Y.:
Sutton Place, East River bank design, October 1927, project

Oak Park, Ill.:
Open Air Auditorium and parkway development plan, August 1925, project*

Ottawa and Hull, Ont.:
Federal Capital plan, June 1912-January 1915*

Palm Beach, Fla.:
City Plan, 1929-30 (1930)
Gulf Stream subdivision and polo fields, 1925, project*

Pasadena, Cal.:
City Plan, March 1923-April 1925*
City Hall competition advisor, March 1924*
Civic Center, January 1923
Center of Arts, September 1924, project (with J. H. Lambert)*
Zoning Ordinance, 1923

Phoenix, Ariz.:
City Plan, 1920-21*

Pittsburgh, Pa.:
Point District Plan, 1914, project

Portland, Or.:
City Plan, 1910-12 (1912)*

Port Washington, Long Island, N.Y.:
Subdivision for Vincent Astor, 1926-27, project*

Rockford, Ill.:
Rockford College plan, project

Rock Island, Ill.:
City Plan, 1922

St. Joseph, Mo.:
Civic Center, 1923, project*

St. Paul, Minn.:
City Plan, 1921-22 (1922)*
Kellogg Boulevard, 1929
Zoning Ordinance, 1922*

San Francisco, Cal.:
Balboa (San Mateo Co.), townsite plan, 1906, project (with DHB)*
City Plan, 1904-05 (1905) (with DHB)*
Civic Center plan, 1906-10, project*
Panama-Pacific International Exposition, site plan, 1911-15*

San Juan, P.R.:
Muñoz Rivera Park, March 1925, project (?)*
Capitol grounds landscaping, 1925, project (?)*

Santa Catalina, Cal.:
William Wrigley, Jr., Memorial Tower, 1933*

Tiffin, Ohio:
River front plan, 1919

Vincennes, Ind.:
George Rogers Clark National Memorial, competition advisors and designers of
　　grounds and Lincoln Memorial Bridge, 1928-35*
Cathedral (addition?), 1934

Washington, D.C.:
Chairman, Board of Architects, 1927-37
　　Federal Triangle site plan (with others)*
　　　　Apex Building (Federal Trade Commission)*
　　　　Great Court (project)
　　Botanic Gardens Conservatory*
　　Capitol Grounds Extension, north to Union Station
　　　　between Louisiana and Delaware Avenues*

Winnetka, Ill.:
City Plan, 1917-21 (1921)*

Regional Plans:
North Shore (Chicago environs), c. 1939*
Preliminary Regional Plan of New York and Its Environs, Sector VI report, June 1923*

The Art Institute of Chicago

Committee on Architecture

David C. Hilliard, Chairman
James N. Alexander
Stanley M. Freehling
Bruce J. Graham
Neil Harris
Carter H. Manny, Jr.
Charles H. Shaw
Stanley Tigerman

Trustees

James W. Alsdorf
Mrs. Julian Armstrong, Jr.
Edward H. Bennett, Jr.
Edwin A. Bergman
Bowen Blair
Wesley M. Dixon, Jr.
James L. Dutt
Marshall Field
Stanley M. Freehling
R. Robert Funderburg
Michael Goodkin
Charles C. Haffner III
William E. Hartmann
David C. Hilliard
John H. Johnson
Duane R. Kullberg
Brooks McCormick
H. George Mann
Mrs. Harold T. Martin
Charles A. Meyer
John W. Moutoussamy
Mrs. Charles F. Nadler
Bryan S. Reid, Jr.
Arthur W. Schultz
Edward Byron Smith, Jr.
Barry F. Sullivan
David G. Taylor
Mrs. Theodore D. Tieken
Arthur MacDougall Wood
William Wood Prince
George B. Young

Life Trustees

John Gregg Allerton
Cushman B. Bissell
William McCormick Blair*
Leigh B. Block
Mrs. Eugene A. Davidson
Mrs. Edwin J. DeCosta
Frank B. Hubachek
Miss Louise Lutz
Andrew McNally III
Everett McNear
William A. McSwain
Mrs. C. Phillip Miller
Mrs. Joseph Regenstein
Joseph R. Shapiro
Edward Byron Smith
Warner Arms Wick
Payson S. Wild

*President Emeritus

Ex Officio Honorary Trustees

Jane M. Byrne, Mayor, City of Chicago
Daniel J. Grim, Comptroller, City of Chicago
Raymond F. Simon, President, Chicago Park District
William Swezenski, Treasurer, Chicago Park District

Ex Officio Trustees

E. Laurence Chalmers, Jr., President,
    The Art Institute of Chicago
James N. Wood, Director,
    The Art Institute of Chicago

Officers

Arthur W. Schultz, Chairman of the Board
Bowen Blair, Vice-Chairman and Treasurer
Marshall Field, Vice-Chairman
Bryan S. Reid, Jr., Vice-Chairman
George B. Young, Vice-Chairman
E. Laurence Chalmers, Jr., President
James N. Wood, Director
Donald J. Irving, Director of the School
Robert E. Mars, Vice-President for Administrative Affairs
Larry Ter Molen, Vice-President for Development and Public Relations
Sharon L. Burge, Secretary